Edward Everett Hale

Our new crusade

A temperance story

Edward Everett Hale

Our new crusade
A temperance story

ISBN/EAN: 9783742826800

Manufactured in Europe, USA, Canada, Australia, Japa

Cover: Foto ©Andreas Hilbeck / pixelio.de

Manufactured and distributed by brebook publishing software (www.brebook.com)

Edward Everett Hale

Our new crusade

OUR NEW CRUSADE.

A Temperance Story.

By EDWARD E. HALE,
AUTHOR OF "IN HIS NAME," ETC.

BOSTON:
ROBERTS BROTHERS.
1875.

Cambridge:
Press of John Wilson and Son.

CHAPTER		PAGE
I.	A Visit to the Deritend	5
II.	The Deritend Attic	30
III.	To Begin at Both Ends	40
IV.	At the Top	60
V.	At the Bottom	69
VI.	Can We, and How?	89
VII.	Card-Playing and Champagne	101
VIII.	Seven Men of Honest Report	112
IX.	Walking and Talking	131
X.	Phi Nu	139
XI.	Word to Pittsburg	157
XII.	The Deritend Club	168
XIII.	The Social Revolution	187
XIV.	Christmas Day	232
XV.	Two by Two	265
XVI.	Bromwich To-Day	281

well as they might. Mrs. Gregg explained that her husband was away from home. The truth was, he had fled, as he always did, from any responsibility. But she said Horace and Frank were at home, and that it would be better for the ladies to see them than to see her husband; so, if Aunt Lois pleased, she would send for them. Aunt Lois did please, and Clara went for the young men. She did not return; and as soon as Fanny got a chance, she slipped away also.

Well, Aunt Lois had made up her mind to do this thing, and she did it. "You know what we have come for, Mr. Gregg," said she, after the introductions. "We really want to persuade all the saloon-keepers, and all the public-house-keepers, to give up selling liquors, and we do not choose to begin with those little Irish holes. We want to begin with you, or, rather, we want to persuade you to begin. Your house is a respectable house, and we want your influence and example."

Pretty well done, Aunt Lois, with that grave young fellow looking you right in the eye, without once winking all the time!

I knew all these young men, — and probably every undergraduate in college did, — Aunt Lois did not know them apart, nor even knew how many they were, nor whether they were Greggs, or were brothers, or cousins, or clerks, or what; nor till to-day had she cared. Besides all these Greggs, there was Mr. Charles Gregg, whose name was on the top of the hotel register, — rather a showy, fussy, incompetent-looking sort of man, who had probably followed the old law of American social life, and "kept tavern" because there was nothing else that he could do. This theory, long since abandoned in great centres, lingers in some such country towns as ours.

Aunt Lois's Committee was not a bad one. For talking power, I think it relied upon her; nor was this a bad reliance. They had met punctually at eleven, and had called in force, all five of them, at the Deritend. They had asked first for the ladies; and in a moment poor Mrs. Gregg, a good deal frightened, came in to them. She was all ready, too. In a few more minutes Clara and Fanny had come in, — nervous, but courteous, and evidently determined to make things pass off as washed the tea-cups in her nice little table-tub, she began to tell us, of her own accord, the funny things that had happened in the interview with the Deritend people, then the more serious things, and at last the sad things; and before the evening was over, in the intervals between visitors and the mail and letter-writing, we had all talked over the Deritend business, in a dozen different forms.

The Deritend House was kept by the Greggs. Precisely who all the Greggs were, I do not suppose Aunt Lois knew before she went there. But she knew some of them. For Mrs. Gregg, a tired, pale-looking woman, and Clara Gregg and Fanny Gregg, two tall and very handsome girls, came regularly to church with a little Gregg boy; and one or all of these ladies often came to the Sewing Society, though not regularly. None of them came to the Temperance Union, as how should they, when Mr. Gregg kept the Deritend House? Then there were two or three young men, whom you saw about the house, and sometimes saw driving the Gregg girls out. Indeed, at any very large party, the Gregg girls would generally bring one of these brothers. But, though three-fourths of the viands named, and trusted to luck that his few guests would not ask for half what were left. For the Deritend kept up the respectabilities as well as it could, but really was an institution to be pitied, rather than to be blamed. For it was anchored at this corner, where there was a certain work to do, having been itself formed and ordered for work utterly different. So have I seen a good woman, who would have kept a comfortable boarding-house with pleasure to herself and to its inmates, made wretched because she was left to be a fine lady with nothing to do; and I have seen a woman, who would have done very good service as a baroness or countess with plenty of money to spend, made wretched in her turn because she kept a boarding-house badly, and knew she did. Such was the Deritend.

Well, at supper I think Aunt Lois was more cheerful, or at least made an effort to appear so. Nobody asked what had happened at the Deritend House; but it was clear enough that the Committee to which she belonged had done its duty, and that that weight was off her mind. As she

There it stood fronting the Common, cornerwise from the Methodist church, — a great ugly brick house, which had once been painted; a monument of the old turnpike days, when there were six stages out of Cumberland which stopped here for breakfast every day, and six stages into Cumberland which stopped here for supper, and any number of emigrant wagons, the summer through, of which the horses were fed in the Deritend stables. It had unfortunately outlived the emigrant days and the turnpike days. The piazzas were rotting down; but no one had any money to renew their steps, or even their planking. The wires of the bells were breaking from year to year; but the proprietors had long ceased to pay for repairs, and the lessees could not think of bell-wires. The paint, as I said, was wearing off. Still the Deritend, which was really a third-class inn, pretended to be a "first-class hotel." It had no sign, for instance. A truly "first-class hotel" never does have one. It still used printed bills of fare for dinner, many thousand being left from some old administration. From these Horace Gregg scored off with his pen every day son that she was low-spirited at breakfast, when the day came for them to visit the Deritend.

You were never at the Deritend? Then you can never have come to Bromwich without an invitation from one of the professors' families to come direct to his house. For the Deritend House is the only tolerable hotel in the town. Mrs. Grundy has always said that, if the professors were not so hospitable, the Deritend would be a better hotel; but that the college folks chose to invite all the "better travel" to their own houses, and none but commercial travellers, otherwise called "drummers," and even less profitable visitors, are left for the public entertainment. As to this, I know nothing. I had never slept in the Deritend, nor so much as bought a cigar there, nor borrowed a toothpick, before the morning of Aunt Lois's visit. Yet I also should have been taken aback, had I gone down town, and seen the Deritend closed. It was a public necessity, there was no doubt of that; but it was a public necessity which neither I nor mine ever cared about, or for which we ever lifted a finger.

I was not at home at dinner; and, as it proved, few of the rest of them were. When I did come home an hour before tea-time, as I sat on the veranda with Bernard, he told me why Aunt Lois had looked dull at breakfast.

The day had come at last when the committee of ladies, appointed by our Woman's Christian Temperance Union, to wait on all the liquor-sellers in town, was to divide itself into its sub-committees, and go about its disagreeable business. Aunt Lois, as being the wife of Dr. Claridge, who was so long the president of our college, is almost, of course, the president of the Union. Whether Aunt Lois would herself have moved the appointment of committees to wait on the tavern-keepers, I do not know. But women stand by each other; and when the Union had voted the committees, and had made the president chairman, she did not shirk, even if she did shrink. When the great committee divided itself into sub-committees, the sub-committee to visit the Deritend House was of course most important, and first named. And of this sub-committee Aunt Lois was the chairman. That was the rea-

OUR NEW CRUSADE.

CHAPTER I.

A VISIT TO THE DERITEND.

I HAD observed at breakfast that Aunt Lois had looked dull.

Every one else had observed it, though of course no one said so. She gave us all our coffee, she pretended to take her own fried potatoes and omelette, but she ate nothing, and she said nothing. Now this is quite unusual with Aunt Lois. Generally, she keeps the children in order, carries on half the talk, sees that no cup is empty, and eats her own breakfast, all at the same time; and this with magnetism that nothing can resist, or, if you please, with life which quickens the whole company.

But this morning there had been no doubt but that Aunt Lois looked dull.

He said, in reply, that he and his brother were very much obliged for the visit, as he was sure his mother and sisters were; that it was much better to speak face to face than it was behind people's backs; that it was not, however, the first time this proposal had been made to him and his brothers; and he begged Aunt Lois and the ladies to believe that they had considered it very seriously, so that his answer, though prompt, was in no sort unconsidered.

"I do not say that we should agree with you, madam, whether a traveller has or has not the right to expect to find a glass of beer, a bottle of sherry, or a glass of brandy, at a hotel. Nor do I ask you to argue that.

"Nor do I think we should agree on another question,—whether the chances for the temperance of any man in this town would not be better, if he came to drink such liquors as we sell at our bar than if he went to drink poisoned whiskey at such holes as you speak of. I do not think we should agree about these questions, and so we will not open them.

"All I need say is, that I am sorry you are

so tired of your neighbors that you want us to leave town. Simply this is what your kind proposal amounts to."

Aunt Lois was really shocked, — not hurt, but puzzled and shocked. She must have explained herself badly, and she began all over again. Everybody knew that the Deritend was much better kept than it had ever been kept, she said. Everybody spoke pleasantly of Mr. Gregg and all the Greggs. She was sure that people were sorry not to see them more. Certainly she had not meant to say any thing so rude. If she had, Mr. Gregg must forget it, and must pardon her. But what she and her friends wanted was a temperance house. Nobody could keep such a house better than Mr. and Mrs. Gregg could, she was sure; and just what the Union hoped was, that they would undertake it.

Horace Gregg smiled gravely, the first time he had smiled in the whole business.

"Indeed, Mrs. Claridge, you have not been rude. I think you cannot be rude. If you had not explained yourself as well as you have, still I should have understood it all. But you do not

A VISIT TO THE DERITEND.

remember that I and my brothers have gone over all this a thousand times. It is our business to go over it, — our first duty; and, indeed, we have done that duty. But it all amounts to this: You and the ladies of the Union, and all the nicer people in Bromwich, want to have the Deritend kept open. You want to have our coach at the station whenever a train comes in, day or night: some of you might be there, or some of your friends. You want to have our dining-hall ready any day of the year for guests, with servants enough, and a proper bill of fare. For although you never come here yourselves, yet the fathers and mothers of the college boys come, and the college boys themselves must be seen to before they are admitted. At Commencement and Class Day, and whatever, you want to have those people provided for whom you do not care to invite to your own houses. And you want the Deritend open for this. All these are public purposes, which make it desirable for Bromwich to have a first-class hotel here. But when it comes to the compensation for rendering these services, — which you know are important, — why, you want us to give up the only source of revenue which the Deri-tend House can rely upon. There is one perfectly regular source of income; but you ladies do not like the method by which it is attained. Very good. You have a right to your tastes and your opinion. Only, as I said, if you ask us to give up that source of income, you ask us to close this house, and to go to some other Bromwich, where people who take the sweet are willing to take the bitter."

It was a long speech; but Aunt Lois liked it; and she liked the dignity and frankness with which the young man spoke to her. She told him so, and then she went on:—

"But surely there are 'temperance houses,' Mr. Gregg. I am sure there are. There is one in Albany, I know. There is one in Syracuse: I saw the sign last month."

"You saw the sign, Mrs. Claridge, but you did not stop there; nor did Dr. Claridge. I think you never spent the night in a temperance hotel in your life, Mrs. Claridge. A temperance hotel is a house where, instead of a woollen carpet on the floor, there is a worn-out canvas; where, if you asked for a newspaper, they would tell you they took none; where your steak at breakfast would be such as Dr. Claridge never saw; where your coffee would be made out of beans ten times burned. Before the Deritend becomes such a house as that, Mrs. Claridge, my father will have ceased to be the landlord."

Now here, as Aunt Lois confessed, Mr. Horace Gregg carried too many guns for her; and, what is more, his guns were too heavy for her. She had, for many years, given up all use of wine or other liquors, because she found that by her abstinence she had much more effect with the college boys, with her servants, and with a hundred other people whom she would persuade to give up their wretched indulgences. There was no sham when she became president of the Temperance Union, though it was a total abstinence society; nor had the Doctor to alter, by a hair's breadth, the customs of his life or home, lest the most critical village gossip should charge him or Aunt Lois with inconsistency. But when Horace Gregg told her that she and the Doctor did not encourage temperance hotels in travelling, she knew he told the truth. And when he said that, while the Union wanted to have the bar of the Deritend given up, she and all the members of the Union were using every day the conveniences which the Deritend supplied, she knew he spoke the truth again.

She was brave enough to acknowledge to Mr. Gregg that his shot had hit, and took advantage of her concession to enter right into the matter as a practical matter, from his point of view, and not from her own. The four other members of the Committee were probably surprised, but they had the wit to be silent. Mrs. Gregg was a lady, and had the sense to be silent too. So Horace Gregg and Aunt Lois had the talk all to themselves, with occasional assistance from Frank Gregg, when he saw a chance to put in a word.

But, after all, nothing came of it, she said. She had thought to press the Greggs by asking them whether, on their own ground, it was fair to make so large a profit as they did, in selling very dear what they bought very cheap? if it was fair to sell at ten cents a glass of liquor, which did not cost them one cent a gill? But Horace Gregg, in his grand way, had said that he need not explain to her that nothing would be gained by anybody, if he undersold the market; that, if he sold liquor at five cents the glass, the Committee would not really be better pleased with the Deritend House than it was now. "Indeed, Mrs. Claridge," said he, "I think you will understand that precisely the pressure which is brought to bear on this business increases its profits, so long as the business lasts. You have read Paley. You remember he says that ballet-dancers have to be paid the more highly, because the occupation they engage in is disreputable. It is just the same with bar-keepers. That is a law of society."

Once more Aunt Lois was a little surprised; this time to have Paley quoted to her in a tavern. But she was pleased in proportion; and, not to tell in its detail all that passed between her and the Greggs, the end of the Committee's visit was a long and sufficiently amicable talk, quite in detail sometimes, as to the ups and downs of such an establishment as the Deritend House. What part of the business paid, and what did not pay, Frank Gregg told openly. He even asked Aunt Lois, with a sort of simplicity which pleased her as much as Horace's gravity did, if she would not like to see how he kept the books and managed the wages' accounts. This she declined. "But the upshot of it all is," said she, "that the liquor business is what supports that house. They make four thousand dollars a year clear profit out of it; and there would not be any Deritend House, if they did not get that four thousand dollars somewhere. Well, as Horace Gregg, said, they could move away. But somebody else would keep the house, who would keep a worse bar than they do, — if one bar can be worse than another, and I suppose it can." And, as Aunt Lois told us this, she really cried with vexation to think that, being in the right, as she knew she was, — willing to make sacrifices, too, as we all knew she was, — strong in a great purpose, and with no small share of the moral power of the community behind her, — she was none the less foiled in that purpose by miserable laws of trade, and by the strength of the tightly knitted web-work of human society.

The Greggs, if you only accepted their point of view, which she knew was wrong, had behaved perfectly all the way through. They had been courteous; they had even been sympathetic and confidential. And Horace Gregg, as the Committee came away, had said in so many words, "You ladies have hit the mark precisely, as you always do. If Bromwich wants us to give up our bar, we will gladly do what Bromwich wants, if only you will show us how to replace the income of four thousand dollars, which giving up the bar will cost us. And, indeed, as I think my brother said, Mrs. Claridge, we will make as large a sacrifice in that matter as anybody in town will."

With such courteous words — words not spoken in defiance, but words which seemed to close the business fatally — had the interview with the Committee ended.

"It seems to me," said my cousin Susie, after Aunt Lois had finally told the story to this critical end, on our pressing instances, "it seems to me that the thing we ought to do is this " ——

What it was, I do not know; nor does anybody else know.

For, if a bomb-shell had exploded under the library table, I think the little company of us would not have been more amazed than at that moment we were.

The door was opened by Martha, the servant-girl, and William Gadsden came in !

WILLIAM GADSDEN !

"Why should he not come in?" says the innocent reader. Is not this a free country? May not a man ring any door-bell he pleases, and walk into any library or drawing-room he pleases? At the least, he can say he wants an autograph.

Dear reader, you do not know who William Gadsden was. William Gadsden had been a law-student in the law-school at Bromwich. A wide-awake, intelligent, nay, a conscientious and religious man he seemed to be. He had come to our house a great deal when Dr. Claridge was the president of the college, because the college and law-school were all one, both being parts of the same paper University. All of us liked Will Gadsden. And he, — ah! did he not like Susie? and Susie, — ah! did not she like him? But —

what a fatal but! — Will Gadsden would drink a little, a good deal, a great deal, as the girls say when they pull out the white leaves from a Marguerite. And at last, — all this was two years before, — at last Will Gadsden broke down — horribly and disgracefully! I myself, who write these words, had watched with him one night in Graduates' Hall, when he was crazy with delirium tremens, and when I thought he would not live until morning. Dr. Claridge had had to send one of the real saints of the college with him to his poor mother's house in Frederick. His father was dead long before. And dear Susie! Ah me! what had Susie suffered, or what had she not suffered? She never told me. And Aunt Lois never told me. And I do not know. Were they engaged before he went? Do not ask me. I do not know. All I know is, that after he went Susie seemed to me like what I imagine a vestal. She was in the world, but not of the world. She was at every pic-nic, at every party. She buttered bread for the children, if we went to Blannerhassett Island. She waltzed with the Freshmen, if there were a party at Madam Wassell's. She cut flannels with the notables, if there were a call for clothing for the 78th Regiment. She took her class of hobble-de-hoys — unfledged men, no longer boys — in the Sunday school. She was the life and fire and glory of the Exclamation Club, which united the nicest girls in Bromich. Yes. But all the same there was not boy or girl, man or woman of us, who would ever have hinted, after Will Gadsden went away, or was sent away in disgrace, that Susie Claridge had one thought of tenderness for any other man, or that it would be well for any other man, though he were King of Hearts, to have one word of tenderness for her! The last time Will Gadsden was in this library, he was so drunk that he told Aunt Lois three times how he had locked himself out of his own room, and Bernard at last had to take him home and put him to bed. That was just before the awful time when the president sent him back to his mother.

And now nobody had heard the door-bell ring; and Martha, pale herself as death, had shown Mr. Gadsden into the room!

Dr. Claridge is a man of the world, though

he was a college president. Aunt Lois is not a woman of the world : but she is what is better, a child of God, self-forgetting and self-sacrificing ; and I never saw nor heard of the exigency that she is not fit for. What Susie is I have tried to tell. What Bernard is you will see. What I am is no matter. For all our varied experience, I confess that, when Will Gadsden came in, we were dashed as much as if Martha had fired off a bombshell under the table. A pause there was, but it lasted only for the least differential of a moment. I will not say that Susie was not the one who rallied first. But it was Aunt Lois who first rose. She half-crossed the room. She did not give Will her hand, nor did he offer his. But she took his hat, and she made him take a chair.

Thank Heaven, there are the stereotyped questions which we all could ask if we were at the stake: When did he come? By what line did he come? Had he expected to come? Had he not been in Europe? We had seen his name in the list of passengers. When Aunt Lois said this, I knew she was getting her wind, as the ungodly say, and was coming up to time. For this was a delicate intimation that we had no means of knowing of his whereabouts but by the newspapers.

Will Gadsden answered every question quite fully, as if he knew that for all parties it was a good thing to gain time, if they meant to regain self-possession. He went quite carefully into his stay in Europe: how he took chambers at the New Inn, in London, and read law there; how he studied civil law in Heidelberg. No. He had not gone as far as Italy. He had put that off till another time. This time he went for work, and for nothing else. Yes, he had seen Gansevoort and Melvin in Heidelberg. He thought they would stay a year longer. He wondered they did not write to old friends.

Really Will Gadsden spun out Europe very well. And Aunt Lois, who was always mollified a great while before she ought to be, began to feel quite at ease with him, and asked at last how he left his mother and sister. And here was the place where the talk ceased to be fencing, and both parties dropped their guard.

"I ought to have said, first of all, that mother

sends her very best love to you,—to all of you." He did not trust himself, even now, to look at Susie. "Mother and I and the little ones have been at Bath all the summer. You know it is a droll old-fashioned Virginia watering-place, where they have tournaments and no end of nonsense. Either the waters did her good, or, as I believe, having no housekeeping did her good. Any way, she is stronger and better than I have seen her for ten years. I have just got them well home; and it is she who has given me courage to show myself here. Indeed, she sent me here. And what I came here to-night for was to give her love, and all her other messages to you — and to Miss Susie." This time he did not say and "to all of you." But he did not look at Susie, and his face was as white as death as he spoke.

Dear Aunt Lois! she is always ten times too forgiving. She said what she never should have said, without asking the Doctor's advice: —

"I am so glad you came! It seems like old times to see you; and do you mean to stay?"

Will Gadsden was already standing, as if to take his leave, though the call had not lasted ten minutes. So unlike the times when he spent half a day at that house on occasions! "Oh, yes! I am going to finish the Law course here, and take my degree, if I can pass your examinations." This with a smile, as if Bromwich examinations were not much to be dreaded after those of Heidelberg. "I was only in the law-school here five months, all told, before. And then," after the least possible pause, "I lost my character here, and it is here that it must be regained, if it is regained at all."

And then the brave fellow smiled, with an exquisite smile of hope and of resolution, which might have been the smile of the archangel Abdiel!

I believe it was that smile which made the Doctor come to the front, — Dr. Claridge, I mean. He had been very pusillanimous before, as most men are, when there are women at hand, in occasions of trial; and he had left Aunt Lois to take the brunt of the action. But he was so pleased with Gadsden's firmness that he said now with real cordiality, "Have you taken your room?"

"Why, no, — or rather yes," said Will, a little gravely. "I wrote to the Steward to ask for my old room, or any thing else in the dear old den. But the Steward says he has nothing vacant. You are growing quite too popular, Doctor Claridge, with all your University improvements, unless you build us some new dormitories. So I have agreed this afternoon with Horace Gregg to let me have one of his dormer-window attics on Bow Street, in the west wing of the Deritend. I expect my books by the freight train of to-night, and to-morrow I shall go to work putting up my shelves, and getting ready for business." And so the proud young fellow bowed and withdrew. Neither Dr. Claridge nor Aunt Lois, and of course not I, had asked him if he would not call again. Far less had Susie!

But Bernard put on his hat, when Will went away, and walked down the street with him. And when Will bade him good-by at the door of the Deritend, Bernard said he had a call to make there, and he went in too.

CHAPTER II.

THE DERITEND ATTIC.

Aunt Lois had certainly not intended to make a second visit at the Deritend within twenty-four hours. But man proposes, and God disposes. As soon as breakfast was over the next morning, Aunt Lois girded herself for a walk, — a most unusual thing for her at the time when housekeepers generally "step round" at home, — and she walked down the hill. Where she was going she had told no one, unless it were her husband; certainly she did not tell the girls nor me.

But it was to the Deritend that she directed her way, and this time as eagerly as yesterday unwillingly.

She asked for Mr. Gadsden, and said they need not call him downstairs, but that she would see him in his room. She climbed the four flights of stairs, — monuments of long-past prosperity, —

passed through the dark and dusty and snuffy entries, knocked at No. 73, and was admitted by Will's ready "Come in!" And this time it was he who was amazed by an unexpected arrival.

Will was sitting on a trunk in the middle of the room, shaping with his jack-knife a wedge which was to play some fundamental part in the support of the book-shelves which leaned, in a paralytic angle, against the wall. The floor was littered with his chips, with the newspapers that had packed his books, and with straw from his other packing-cases. The whole apartment was the very concrete embodiment of confusion worse confounded. There were three or four cane chairs stacked together in one corner; there was a rough roll of carpet in another, with two or three dirty window-shades which had been tumbled over it. The bed was not yet made up for the day; and a dressing-gown of Gadsden's, a pair of pantaloons, and other apparel, lay upon it. He started to his feet, — half-laughing and half-dismayed, — offered his hand to Aunt Lois, who did not refuse it, and then with wild and futile gestures he tried to dust out a chair for her to sit in.

"It is ever so good in you to climb up here. But why did not you send up for me?"

Aunt Lois got her breath by degrees. She was half-crying and half-laughing.

"You may charge as much as you please to the account of curiosity," said she. "I did want to see what sort of a burrow you had found. For a burrow, it is near enough to the sky." Then she stopped, and pretended she had not recovered her breath! Ah me! to think that even Aunt Lois made believe sometimes!

"No, Mr. Gadsden, that was not what I came for really. Really I came to say that I cannot bear to have you living in this house! There, that is frank; and you like frankness."

The great tears came to Will Gadsden's eyes. "Mrs. Claridge, if there is a saint this side heaven, that saint is you!"

"Fiddlestick for saints!" said Aunt Lois. "I am the mother of two boys and of four girls, Mr. Gadsden; and, though I have never seen your mother, I know how to feel for a mother like your mother, who has only one daughter and one son." Here she dropped her voice a little, but she looked him in the eye more steadily than ever; and she went on: "I know I should be wretched if a son of mine took rooms in a drinking-house like this, Mr. Gadsden! That is the reason why I want you to come away."

"Thank you, dear Mrs. Claridge! thank you ten thousand times over for saying it; nay, for caring enough for me to come and say it. Thank you, and thank you again and again. If you say so, when you have heard me through, I will leave my airy 'burrow;'" and he laughed. "Nay, if you say so, when you have heard me through, I will leave Bromwich; and I will open my office in Columbus to-morrow, as I can do, for I can enter at the bar at any moment I choose. But I think what I said last night holds water. In Bromwich I lost my character, and in Bromwich I will regain it. Carry that statement a little farther, dear Mrs. Claridge: in the Deritend House I lost it, and in the Deritend I mean to find it."

She wanted to speak, but he would not let her. "Pardon me one moment more," said he. "You think I am over-straining a set of new-formed resolutions. Let me tell you first what I am, and what I know I can do. My dear mother took me home, when Ned Morrill brought me back to Frederick from here,—well, as only a man's mother can, Mrs. Claridge! She nursed me,—you know how she nursed me. She sent for Longcross,—he's our doctor,—the noblest and the wisest and the truest old brick that ever lived. And he nursed me, too, and he fed me, and he counselled me—yes, he ordered me. If it were not for him, Aunt Lois,—I beg your pardon, but you know you used to let me say so,—if it were not for him, Mrs. Claridge, I should not be here to-day. Well, dear Mrs. Claridge, I did what he bade me. I should as soon have deceived an archangel, and as soon disobey one. He sent me to London, and told me what to do there; he advised me to go to Heidelberg, and told me how to do it, and what to do there. What he bade me do I have done. And, first of all, and last of all, now for two years and three months I have neither tasted nor touched any sort of liquor,—not beer in Heidelberg, not sherry in London. I do not say I have never been tempted; but I do say I have met the temptation. And, at least, you know that I tell you the truth."

She wanted to speak; but again he would not let her.

"One moment more. I have such reason for thinking that I can hold to a resolution which involves life or death for me. I know that as well as you do, — better. And I know one thing more, which you may not have thought of.

"Unless I am trying to help some one else out of this pit, I shall certainly fall in again myself.

"That is the eternal law. If I am brooding about my own failure or my own success, I shall certainly go to the bad, Mrs. Claridge. The doctor told me that, and, if he had not told me, I should have found it out before I had been in London a fortnight.

"Knowing that, I knew that if I came to Bromwich I must find somebody somewhere whom I could help from something, or that I was gone.

"And so when Mr. Dumesnil wrote me that there was no room for me in the old den, it flashed across me that there would be room here. And I thought this, Aunt Lois, — do not think me too bold for thinking it: I thought if I am here at dinner and at supper, every day, you know, — in and out, you know, as a man must be, who has his room here, — I thought I should have a chance to say something, maybe to do something, for the boys who loaf in here, just as I used to do; such as no other man could well have, — any way, I thought I would try."

His face blazed with animation; and now he stopped, and waited her answer.

But it was a minute before she spoke. "My dear boy," she said then, "I dare not say, I do not know; but, if I had spoken at the first minute, I believe I should have said, God in his mercy sent you. Mr. Gadsden, what do you suppose was the last visit I made yesterday, — before you saw me at our house? Of course you cannot guess. It was a visit on Horace and Frank Gregg, in the ladies' drawing-room downstairs. I had come to ask them to give up the bar at this house."

"No!" cried he, surprised in his turn. "And what did they say?"

"They said that to ask them to do that was to ask them to remove their mother and their sisters out of town. They said that, if there was to be a hotel here, it needed so many servants, and so much fuel, and so large a meat-bill, and so on, — in dollars and cents. They said that the bar alone made a clear and sure profit on the investment made, and that without that profit the house must be closed. They not only said this, Mr. Gadsden, but they proved it."

"I suppose they did. I suppose they did," said Will Gadsden, slowly. "Do you know I have thought more and more, these six months, that we must begin at the other end."

"Unless we begin at both ends," said Aunt Lois, after another long pause.

"Unless we begin at both ends!" repeated he, cheerfully and thoughtfully.

"And now," continued Aunt Lois, "I will not say one word more about what brought me here. I came to beg you, by all that was holy, by your mother's love, by your memory of your father, and by all your hopes for your own life, — I came to beg you to leave this house, this day and this hour. I was going to tell you where you could go, — that you could have one of Mrs. Fordyce's rooms, — a thousand times better than this, of course, in every way. I was going to say, — well, Mr. Gadsden, I was going to say that, if you could not pay Mrs. Fordyce's rates, I could and I would." And the tears stood in Aunt Lois's eyes. "And now see what a weather-cock I am! I am like the Abbot in the 'Lord of the Isles.' I go away begging you to stay, — if only you are wholly sure, to stay and to conquer. May God himself be with you, and be your strength." Here she broke down crying. Nor was Gadsden much firmer.

"Only, my dear child," said she, "you must not stay in such a Dom-Daniel as this. I must have Margaret Flynn here to put down this carpet, and John David to put up these curtains, and Mrs. Gregg must send up somebody to wash these windows, and these detestable fly-papers must come down."

"O dear Mrs. Claridge, do leave something for the rest of the world to do. I shall have order made out of chaos one day here, and you shall come and see my miracles."

"Well, at least, you will come and dine with us to day!"

The young man's face fired crimson. "Not to-day! No! not for many, many days, Mrs. Claridge. Remember what I am doing, and what I have to do. Let us begin at the beginning!"

CHAPTER III.

TO BEGIN AT BOTH ENDS.

THAT afternoon the general committee met in the ladies' parlor of the Methodist Church, to hear the report of their sub-committee. No fag-end meeting was this, — attended only by the elect, who had nothing else to do, — but well-nigh every woman was there who had any right to be there, and some, I should say, who had no right. "Important meeting," it said on the card : true enough; but the women went, not only because it was important, but because they were curious to know what had happened.

At such meetings there is generally great pretence of parliamentary order, with an utter defiance, from sheer ignorance, of parliamentary rules : many motions are made, back and forth, which are never regularly put to vote ; and then, out of a chaos which would drive Cushing or Bentham or Jefferson or Romilly crazy, there comes a "sense of the meeting," as clear and as well formulated as ever was drawn up by a Quaker clerk. This remark will displease Mrs. Howe. Still, I commend it to her serious reflection. " Paradoxical as it is, it is nevertheless true."

The full committee meeting at the Methodist church was no exception to the rule. When Aunt Lois wanted silence, that they might hear Miss Ann Haldemand's report, they all broke up in groups, and talked in groups. When, on the other hand, she asked the different sub-committees to separate and put on paper the heads of their recommendations, everybody sat still in her seat; and Mrs. Featherstone made a very interesting statement about what she had noticed in the vine-growing regions of Central France. All the same, being "clear sheer determined," or, as the vernacular says, "sot" in their plans, the committee advanced through its afternoon business, though by ways it had not known. The sub-committees, sooner or later, brought in their reports. Aunt Lois told what I have told you about the "Deritend." The others told about the "Eagle," the "Northern," and what Flynn said, and what

Mrs. Schumann said; and how they could not get in at the saloon by the canal lock; and how they believed the people had moved away from the shop below Bailey's, — at least the curtains were down, and nobody seemed to know any thing.

There had not been much gained in any of the interviews. George Readhead, at the "Northern," had said he would give up his bar if all the rest would. But even Mrs. Morris, who reported this, saw that it meant nothing. For the rest, the different dealers had been civil enough; but some had been defiant, some had been silent, and nobody had made any concession. The ladies were disposed at first to fall back on the satisfaction of thinking and saying that nobody had expected any thing from this appeal. But if any motion would have been made or not, I do not know; for, in connection with the bar at the "Northern," Mrs. Oelrich fell to telling of the "wretched times" she had had the last week with Corkery, their "man of all work," — that same bright fellow whom everybody remembered; who, indeed, drove in the carry-all last week when she came to the meeting.

Mrs. Oelrich was Gustav Oelrich's wife. He is the great leather man out at Faff's Mills. They have a beautiful place there,—greenhouse and carefully kept garden; and they have so many guests of their own, that they might be quite independent of our Bromwich society. But Gustav Oelrich is a public-spirited man, who does not shirk his share of the public duties of the borough. They always come into church, and stay to both services. And Mrs. Oelrich, who is an American, and not a German, takes more pains than you might think to keep up social relations not only with the college people, but with all the village. She is at the Sewing Circle, at the Shakespeare Club, subscribes to the Reading Club, and, in short, insists on being counted in in all our village plans and sociabilities. So she is a general favorite with us; and her good sense and real generosity help things very vigorously along.

Corkery, on whom the conversation diverged, after the report on the bar at the "Northern," was what in other social order would be called a "coachman." Nobody called him a coachman at Faff's Mills,—perhaps because there was not a coach within three miles. He had the oversight of the stable, he took Mrs. Oelrich's orders, into town every day for her purchases, and brought out the mail; he was responsible for all the hay and corn and oats, and such things; he would have done any thing in the garden that Miss Bertha asked him to; and if he had been told to take the boys chestnutting, he would have gone, with entire satisfaction to all persons concerned. So that in the village we should have said he was the Oelrichs' "man,"—that is what we should have called him. Not but Gustav Oelrich hired a hundred other "men," and paid them every Saturday night. For all that, they were his "hands," his "help," his "operatives," or what you please. Corkery was the Oelrichs' "man."

And Corkery was well-nigh faultless in his vocation. Gustav Oelrich used to say that he would double his wages, and settle them on him for life, if — if only he would agree to have his semi-annual "sprees" at fixed times; would give notice three days beforehand; have the spree and be done with it, and come back to duty after it was over. It was the lawless and wholly incalculable moment of the spree that drove Gustav Oelrich to despair. Corkery drove the girls into town one winter night to a ball; and when twelve o'clock came, and the last dancer had gone, eight inches of snow on the ground, and more falling, there was no Corkery and no carriage. Walter Wiltse had to find his father's carriage and drive them home himself, — with his "white kid gloves on," Oelrich always said; but this was an exaggeration. And now Corkery had pulled the string of his shower-bath for the last time. The day he brought Mrs. Oelrich in to the last meeting had been his last day. That morning he had asked that the two Shepherd boys who worked in the stable might go to Oneida County, because their father was dead, and he had got permission. He and the gardener were to take care of the horses. That night, by way of strengthening himself for these extra duties, he had gone down to the "Northern;" had been seen there by some of the tannery people; and that was the last of Corkery. Nobody to see to the horses but John, who did not know Redjacket's harness from Kate's, and who had already had his foot trodden on by Redjacket, so that he could hardly stand. Mr. Oelrich was very angry; he had told Corkery that he would never take him back again if he had another spree, and he never would. Bertha Oelrich had driven in the bays that afternoon. "I was afraid for my life," Mrs. Oelrich said; "but I thought I had one report to bring, if nobody else had any. So I made my will and came; and here we are. How we are to get home, I am sure I do not know."

At this moment Mrs. Oelrich was called out, and Bertha took up the wondrous tale of Corkery, and what they did without him, — all the ladies of her mother's age and standing drawing their chairs as closely up as they could to listen; and a very funny story Bertha made of it in her bright way.

Mrs. Oelrich returned, — all amazement. Had she been laughing or crying? She was laughing now, but you could not tell. "Well," said she, "you may talk of an angel, and you hear the flap of his wings! Who do you think called me out? Who, to be sure, but John Corkery himself! or a very gentlemanly looking person who brought him. This gentleman said that Corkery wanted to come to ask my pardon, and Mr. Oelrich's; and sure enough there, in the boy's library, was my man, waiting for me."

It was even so. John Corkery had pulled through his spree. He had been ashamed to go near Gustav Oelrich's house. He had not a cent of money. He had not so much as a coat to his back, for he had pawned the very coat he wore with a worthless broker we had then in Bromwich. Freezing, starving, ashamed beyond words, hating liquor, hating himself, hating life, he had fallen in with a man named George Ruther, the " gentlemanly-looking person," who had brought him to Mrs. Oelrich. Corkery had known perfectly well that he could never go back to his service there. But Mr. Ruther said that the apology was his own notion, that he said he had disgraced himself more by misusing Mrs. Oelrich's confidence in him than in any other way, and that he must tell her how much ashamed he was, and how sorry he was. And so Mr. Ruther had brought him. John Corkery had been affected to tears, and you may be sure Mrs. Oelrich had. He had begged her pardon; asked her to ask the young ladies to forgive him, and had said he knew Mr. Oelrich never would, or he would go and see him.

What was he going to do?

"I am sure I don't know, ma'am. But Mr. Ruther here, and the rest of them, think they can take care of me. Good-by, ma'am. Would you give this, with John's love, to Master Arthur for me. The little fellow liked to have it to play with sometimes." And he pulled out a gentleman's pocket-knife, which Mrs. Oelrich knew was the joy of his life. It was given him by Colonel Eden of the English sixty-second, when Corkery was his servant in India. And so he hurried away.

"How did he look, mamma?" said Bertha, half-crying too; for Mrs. Oelrich was very much affected as she told the story.

"Look! Oh, he looked as if he had had a fit of sickness. But he was neat, smoothly shaven, and well-dressed. He has fallen among friends. Who is this Mr. Ruther?" And she turned to Mrs. Etter, who knows everybody and every thing in the village.

But even Mrs. Etter was somewhat at fault

here. She thought, however, that he must be one of the new people who had come in with the railroad; and, if he were the man she thought he was, he had a part of a house on one of the new streets, — Worth Street, as you crossed the canal. Her husband would know, and she would ask him.

"What did he mean, mamma, when he said that 'we' would take care of John? Who are 'we'?" This was Bertha's question to Mrs. Oelrich.

Mrs. Oelrich had meant to ask him. But Mr. Ruther had turned away from the interview between her and John, as if he had no right there.

"It seems to me," said Aunt Lois, "that if we could find out who 'we' are, and what 'we' do mean to do about this poor fellow, we should get back to the business of the day. I believe it is providential, the whole of it, Mrs. Oelrich! To think of their coming here just when you were telling the story!"

And thus it was the way that it happened, that, when, half an hour after, one of the younger girls of the society, who was sitting in a group at the window, announced that Jane Ruther and her brother had stopped at Clark and Vandewall's, and that Jane was holding the horse while her brother went into the store, Aunt Lois asked Mrs. Oelrich whether she thought it would do to ask him in for a few minutes to talk with them. Mrs. Oelrich was sure it would do, and in a moment found her hat and shawl, and with Mrs. Etter ran across the street to give the impromptu invitation. In a minute more they appeared with their captive, and with Jane Ruther, — whom the younger girls welcomed as a school-mate.

George Ruther was, indeed, a gentlemanly-looking man; and in this rather trying introduction he bore himself very well. Of course everybody laughed and made fun of the invitation, that the ladies could not get on without at least one gentleman, and all that. Of course, he was introduced to I know not how many heads of committees. Aunt Lois rather gravely apologized for the liberty they had taken, said they would not detain him; got his hat and whip away from him, and made him sit down. Then she told him very briefly what they wanted.

"Mrs. Oelrich says that some friends of yours have got hold of this poor John of hers, and mean to take care of him. Pray how do you go to work with such a man? how ought I to go to work with such a man? and if you have any hope of succeeding with him, on what is that hope founded?"

Bertha Oelrich whispered to her mother, and Mrs. Oelrich followed up Aunt Lois's little speech by saying, "You said *we* were going to take care of him, Mr. Ruther. Who are 'we'?"

Mr. Ruther almost blushed. He looked very handsome, he was so animated; yet he found it somewhat hard to answer so many questions. He began with the last.

"Oh! 'we' are a little knot of friends, not a club exactly, but a sort of club; and one of us fell in with this poor fellow that night, when I believe he might have drowned himself, if Lewis had not taken him home. Lewis is the flag-man at the Ulster crossing. As Lewis went home at midnight, after the night express passed, he stumbled on poor Corkery dead drunk by the roadside. I hope you never saw such a brute,

Mrs. Claridge. Lewis could not lift him, but found Moore, and they two carried him home to Lewis's tenement. Mrs. Lewis made up a bed for him, and they got his boots off, and put him to bed. The next day Lewis came round to me, and since that we have been trying to take care of him."

"'We,' again," said Aunt Lois, smiling: "do you mean that it is the business of your club to take care of drunken men?"

"Oh, not at all, except as it is everybody's business,—yours, and Mr. Gregg's, for instance, at the Deritend. If it really interests you," he said, after a moment's hesitation, "the club, as you call it, is a society which,—well, we are all working-men, who find we cannot do all alone quite what we want to do, so we have this little compact, that we will help each other in such things, and that perhaps was the reason Mr. Lewis and Mr. Moore came to me."

"What do you call the society?"

Again he hesitated a moment; but then said simply: "It is called the 'Wadsworth Brothers.'"

Bertha Oelrich turned full on him: "Are you the men that have the four mottoes?"

"We are a few of them," said he; and he smiled.

Bertha Oelrich had forgotten herself. But she was always impulsive. She took from a chain a gold locket she wore, snapped the case open, and held it out to Mr. Ruther that he might read; and then passed it to the other ladies. On the two open faces of the gold was engraved, —

> "Look up, and not down;
> Look out, and not in."

"Those are two of the Wadsworth mottoes, Mrs. Etter. The other two are on the other side, —

> "'Look forward, and not back;

And, —
> Lend a hand.'"

"It seems to have been the last motto that served our friend Corkery," said Aunt Lois, gravely. "Pray tell us how, Mr. Ruther," — as if she would call back the meeting to its business.

He said there was not much to tell. It was a day or two before Corkery could talk very coherently. He did not want to go out, and Mrs.

Lewis had easily kept him in bed all the time. She felt a good deal relieved when, one morning, he seemed to have a little appetite, and drank off a bowl of broth she brought him. Then nothing would do but he must leave town. He would go to Pittsburg; he would walk there. There was a recruiting station at Pittsburg, and he would enlist. He could never show his face again where Mrs. Oelrich could see him. But Ruther himself, and others of the Wadsworth men, got hold of him. They told him that this was unmanly; that he must stay here till people saw there was something of him; that he was too good a soldier to desert because things did not look well. "We have talked a good deal about it," said Mr. Ruther, finally; "and we have determined to put him in charge of a little enterprise of ours, down at the shop on Front Street, below Bailey's. Probably none of you ladies know the place. It is a drinking-house, and the keeper was sent to the House of Correction last week for stealing a horse. The place is empty, and we are going to fit it up for a sort of reading-room and library, — well, smoking-room and place of general comfort for the poor fellows there whose wives cannot make comfortable homes for them. We shall let them have their pipes, Mrs. Claridge. We are going to have coffee and tea for them, — perhaps something more. Only one thing they shall not have; and that is bad whiskey!" This he said with a flash of anger, which Aunt Lois said seemed almost like Satan!

Mrs. Oelrich said, "like Michael." But this was afterwards.

"And do you really dare to put this broken-down drunkard, who may go on another spree any day, in charge of your enterprise?"

"As to that," said George Ruther, "we must put somebody in charge. But, to tell you the truth, it is John Corkery really who starts the enterprise, or for whom we start it. You can do nothing for such a man unless you give him something to do. Nay, he cannot 'reform himself,' as people call it, unless he engages 'in reforming' others. Nothing is so sure as that he will be drinking again in six months, unless he be at work, and hard at work, to save other people from drinking. Whenever he has the holy horror of a bar-room that — that you ladies have, or that I have, and for the same reason, there is no fear that he will go into one again. That is a long story; but that is really our notion about opening the reading-room. We planned it last winter; but we have never found that things were quite ripe. Just now they seemed ripe. This wretched Sullivan stole the horse, and was sent to jail; so his shop is all ready for us, — just where we wanted our place. But we had no man to keep it. Just then poor John Corkery loses his employment with your husband, madam, and falls in our way; and so we find our man."

"The ladies will please come to order," said Aunt Lois, tapping vigorously with her thimble. "The ladies will come to order! The ladies will be glad to hear that Mr. Ruther reports that one liquor-shop in the village is closed already. The shop below Bailey's, where Mrs. Briscomb and Miss Helen were not able to enter, is to be purified and consecrated, and opened as a reading-room for working-men, without whiskey, by the Wadsworth Brothers."

Quite a little round of applause and congratulation followed this speech, in the midst of which Mr. Ruther recovered his hat and whip, called his sister Jane, and bade the heads of committees good-by. "Please say nothing about the Wadsworth brothers," said he. "It is no secret, but we do not care to be in print." Then, rather louder: "When our reading-room is open, if the ladies walk that way, I hope they will look in. It is for working-women as well as for working-men; and I see you all work while you carry on your discussions." So Mr. George Ruther bowed himself out of the room.

Great buzzing followed, and now the women were talking in earnest, and had something very real to say. "That man has got hold of something," said Mrs. Oelrich, "and you saw his face. He and the people behind him will hold on. How much finer this is than making speeches!"

"But we must have the speeches, too, mamma," said Bertha Oelrich, perhaps a little too abruptly.

"He has got hold of something perfectly definite. He knows what he is about, and these people behind him know what they are about. He will have in twelve months' time a set of workpeople meeting there at his smoking-room who will set the fashion to all the boys, and will give the tone to all the neighborhood, just as that dirty Flynn's saloon now sets the fashion and gives the tone. I made Bertha drive round by your house, Mrs. Etter, just that I might not see Flynn's house. I cannot bear it. And my poor John Corkery is to be the agent in it all! What will Mr. Oelrich say?"

If they had asked me what Mr. Oelrich would say, I could have told them that he would contribute fifty dollars towards the charges of the reading-room, and would never tell anybody a word of what he had done.

But I was not there, and report this only from Susie's and Aunt Lois's narratives.

"There are forty grog-shops in town," exclaimed little Mrs. Briscomb; but I am afraid the town will not support forty reading-rooms," she added, with a dolorous groan that made everybody laugh.

Mrs. Oelrich said, half-aside, that she did not dare propose ten, but she should be sorry to think that the work-people at the railroad were going to have all the reading. "It seems as if, thanks to Mr. Ruther, they would have one convenience that nobody else in town has.

"Mrs. Claridge," she added in a moment, "these gentlemen have begun at the bottom. Might it not be possible

TO BEGIN AT BOTH ENDS?"

But even Aunt Lois did not answer. For the clock had struck for half-past five, and this was not a tea-meeting. The ladies were putting up their work, paying their fines and assessments, and even Aunt Lois was *distrait.*

But as Mrs. Oelrich left, Aunt Lois said to her, "Could not you come in to tea to-morrow evening, and bring Miss Bertha. We can talk there."

As if they had not talked here!

CHAPTER IV.

AT THE TOP.

"WE shall have to make the men help us."

"The men and the boys, the old women and the babies, everybody must help. It is a social revolution."

"What would you call it?"

"That is a hard question, and a very important one."

"You might say the Woman's Club."

"Oh, not in the least!—do not drop a word of that. If it is not a man's club quite as much as it is a woman's club, it will never do at all. And the men must think they originate it all. Do not give an idea, dear Bertha, that it is a woman's club."

Bertha laughed very heartily, and said she would never use those words again. It might be the Centaur's Club, for all her. But she did not think it would amount to much without Aunt Lois and Mrs. Oelrich.

For all these outbursts came in, in the middle of the "talk," when Aunt Lois had the ladies to tea, so that there might be a chance to talk, which, as she said, was well-nigh impossible in the general committee.

"When I was in England last year," said Mrs. Oelrich, "we were at Oxford, and we stayed then at the Clarendon Hotel. Gustav wanted to see the 'London Spectator,' and he asked Mrs. What's-her-name, the landlady, if they had it in the house. 'Oh, certainly,— it was in the club-room: would he come in.'

"I believe she had no right to let him in, but perhaps she knew there was nobody else there.

"Gustav was so pleased that he called me in. There was, on the ground floor, this nice large parlor, as pretty a room as you need see; there was an open fire, real comfortable arm-chairs, and all the newspapers, and all the magazines. My dear, it was a man's club-room, and a very small one at that. But it was the first I was ever in, and for that matter the last.

"I remember Gustav groaned as he came away. 'That is the reason,' he said, 'why men like to live in large towns and cities, and do not like to make leather at Faff's Mills!'

"And just think of it, Mrs. Claridge! What do we live for but to have our lives a little bit bigger this month than they were last month,— to find a wider outlook somewhere? Unless we do that, I do not see that life is worth living for!

"Now, just suppose that the Greggs would let us have those two south parlors at the Deritend, which are now simply hideous. I went there last summer, and took Mrs. Clarke out to our house as soon as she could lock her trunk."

"For which, doubtless, the landlord thanked you," said Dr. Claridge, laughing.

"I did not think of the landlord: I thought of her, sweet soul, and her children!

"Just imagine, I say, a cheerful fire in a gigantic Franklin in each of those fire-places; imagine a cheerful, very warm Brussels on the floor, — something such a carpet as this, Doctor; imagine a dozen or two new novels, and all the new monthlies and weeklies. Imagine me, arrived in town with the bays, and waiting for my husband to come out from some wretched directors' meeting. Suppose for a wonder that I do not choose to come in and bore you or Mrs. Ellery or Mrs. Etter, while I wait for him. Suppose I had rather not talk than talk. Suppose I should go in to this pretty club-room, sit in an easy-chair before the fire, and ring the bell, and tell the girl to bring me a cup of tea. Don't you think I would pay ten dollars a year for the chance to do that thing?"

"I suppose you would," said Dr. Claridge; "but whether one hundred and ninety-nine other ladies would in this neighborhood, I am not sure."

"Nor am I," said the pertinacious lady, not used to giving up her points. "I am quite sure there are not so many women who would ask their husbands for ten dollars to make them perfectly comfortable. But I know one man who would pay; and that is the Rev. Amos Claridge, S.T.D., late President of Barrow College, and Emeritus Professor of Moral Philosophy. He would be 'mighty glad' to see the 'Quarterly,' and the 'Revue des Deux Mondes,' and some of the naughty papers that it does not do for him to subscribe for. Nay, he would not be very sorry to look in just before tea some evening, and find Mrs. Katherine Oelrich, or some other equally agreeable lady sitting there, waiting for her husband to take her home."

The Doctor had to laugh at this appeal, and he owned that she had two subscribers already.

"Bertha will tell you," said the impetuous woman, "that it only needs ten subscribers, through and through in earnest, — *thorough*, as my dear, hateful Lord Strafford says, — to do any thing. Indeed, I believe Abraham found that out long ago, did he not? Doctor, I always come to you for my theology. If ten of us are in earnest, we shall put it through."

Aunt Lois believed in the plan from the beginning. She believed in it all the more from what had passed in the attic of the Deritend between her and poor Gadsden. Both the women had slept on what that clear-headed Ruther had said, and a plan not unlike Mrs. Oelrich's had formed itself among us at the Doctor's even before she came in. More quiet than Mrs. Oelrich, still she said all this very distinctly.

"You see," said that lady, "nothing really great ever fails,—nothing that rests on a principle, as Gustav says. Now this plan does rest on a principle. It rests on this principle, which will work a revolution in society," and she laughed again at her own eagerness.

"The principle is this: that whereas men, when they meet in clubs alone, take to drinking and smoking, and at best play whist or billiards, and at worst play poker or rouge et noir, they would have a thousand times nicer times, and would neither drink nor steal, if they had women with them.

"Do not interrupt me, my dear Doctor! Let me confess that the principle may be stated exclusively thus: that whereas women, when they meet in companies alone, turn back badly on their own lives, and discuss the difficulties of the household and nursery,— as, poor souls, why should they not, seeing they are so much more alone, or away from people of their own age, than men?— when they are with men, they are at their best, talk their best, act their best, teach and learn, and of course enjoy, as they never do and never can in feminine coteries.

"Why, it is no shame to the boys in the college, that, if they knew a hundred nice Bromwich girls had joined in this Clarendon Club of mine, a hundred of them would join it the next day.

"And it is no shame to the girls in Bromwich, that, if they heard that a hundred of the boys in the college had joined it, a hundred of them would join the next day — *if they dared.* Perhaps they will not dare; but with as good a cause as ours behind, Doctor, I believe they will!"

In such fashion the impetuous Mrs. Oelrich went on with her plan, born out of George Ruther's reading-room, for taking the Deritend captive. She had thoroughly digested Aunt Lois's report of the day before: "If we wanted to break up the Deritend bar, we must supply an income of four thousand dollars to the Deritend every year." George Ruther had given her the hint. Here were three hundred women in the Temperance Union. Here were the outlying manufacturers, who would pay a good deal for comfort in Bromwich, even if they would do nothing for temperance. Here were the college students. She had always remembered that cheerful Clarendon Club at Oxford; and she could not help wishing that that, or something better, might be possible at Bromwich.

Her plan was made, to the least corner, when she came in to Aunt Lois's to tea.

She would form a club of gentlemen and ladies, to open club-rooms at the Deritend.

There should be dressing-rooms for the ladies, and a smoking-room for the gentlemen. There should be a reading-room where people might not talk, and a parlor with a piano where they might talk as much as they chose.

"Even if you were playing the Funeral March on the death of a hero," my dear Susie.

There should be honorary members, active members, and silent members. The honorary members should pay $20 a year, or $200 once for all. The active members should pay $10 a year; they should vote, choose officers, and carry the whole through. The silent members should have all the privileges except that of voting.

"They will be the college boys, — and you,

Susie, and Bertha, and other people who do not want to pay more than two dollars. That is what they can pay."

As soon as the club was formed, the president would go to the Deritend, and offer to hire those rooms which Mrs. Oelrich had set her eyes upon, on condition that no bar should be kept in the house, and no license for liquor-selling asked for. On that condition the president should offer to hire and furnish these rooms, and hold out the temptation of bringing to the house the five hundred people most respected in the borough and in the county. And if, to gain the condition, it was necessary, the president was to offer the Deritend House three thousand dollars' rent for the rooms!

"Of course it is more than they pay for the whole house. But it will show we mean work. And for one year we can raise this money, and do this thing.

"For next year, let next year care."

This was Mrs. Oelrich's bold plan.

But, alas! at the same moment, Satan, — or was it Belial? — or possibly Beelzebub, had other plans in view.

CHAPTER V.

AT THE BOTTOM.

BERTHA and Susie were told that they might make a chance to drop a hint about our club to the Gregg girls, and that the Gregg girls might sound their brothers about it.

Mrs. Oelrich was quite willing to have the young men think the matter over before she approached them with any formal proposition. Indeed, it was rather hard to say in what form any proposition could come, or whom it should come from.

For Mrs. Oelrich was like all other inventors who introduce an element wholly new into human society. To form her new stocking, she had to "make believe" once all round, and, for her first row of visible stitches, to knit into stitches which existed only in her imagination.

So Bertha made a chance to sound Fanny Gregg, and Fanny Gregg made a chance to sound her brothers. Both Horace and Frank were interested. Horace thought it all but impossible, but Frank thought it practicable. Any way, they didn't snub their sisters, as the girls had feared they might, but said they would turn it over, and be ready to talk to the ladies, if they would come to them again.

Meanwhile, quite unexpectedly, Bertha Oelrich secured the co-operation of Will Gadsden in the new enterprise. Very much amazed she was to find herself walking with him or talking with him, and much more amazed to find herself in alliance with him. Bertha knew, as every other girl in town knew, the whole story of his delirium tremens, and his disgrace. She did not know, as it happened, what half the girls in town knew, that he had come back to the scene of this disgrace. Susie could have told her, but just then Susie would have died before she would have whispered his name even to Bertha, although Bertha was her dearest friend.

So Bertha was amazed to find herself walking across the Green with him, and, still more, talking to him almost confidentially.

She had left the Deritend after calling on Fanny Gregg, on whom none of the house of Oelrich had ever called before. She was hurrying across the Green, when Will Gadsden met her and touched his hat. Bertha just bowed, as coldly as she knew how.

Will Gadsden, however, turned and followed her. "Let me speak to you, Miss Oelrich, for one moment only. It is about poor John Corkery. My friend, Mr. Ruther, has just left me, and I know he spoke to your mother about him.

"We have opened our reading-room in the old grog-shop: to-night we are to have quite a little festivity at the opening. A good many of the railroad hands will be there, and, I am proud to say, one or two of the old habitués beside poor John himself, who, I am afraid, knew the place only too well. He will be there on duty for the first time. Miss Bertha, it occurred to Ruther, and it occurred to me too, that if your father were driving out of town, and could stop a moment and say an encouraging word to John, it would do him more good than all the rest of us put together, do."

Bertha was all amazed, and upside down. She was walking fast, and he by her. She stopped, and put out her hand, and said, "Thank you, ever so much, Mr. Gadsden. I am almost sure he will, even if he has to drive in on purpose; and I, or my mother, could we come too?"

"Indeed, yes! we should be only too happy," said the handsome fellow, smiling, and looking happy and at ease for the first time in the interview. "A great many of the men's wives will be there, and I know you will be glad to come." And then he would not walk with her a moment more. He retained the whole air of a person who spoke to her on business, and nothing more. He touched his hat again, turned back and walked the other way.

And this with Bertha Oelrich, with whom he had sauntered by the hour by the side of the canal, and danced, by the hour almost, in her father's drawing-rooms!

But that evening Mr. Oelrich and Bertha did come in to the dedication. And Mr. Oelrich talked with John Corkery, man fashion, cordially and kindly. And Bertha Oelrich talked with Mr

Ruther, — talked about the Wadsworth Club, and how she first learned the "four mottoes," about the original ten, and the Kermadeck Islands, and many other things which are to this reader Hebrew.

And then, when Mr. Ruther was called to other guests, she found herself by Will Gadsden, and because she was resolved to break his fence she said to him, —

"So you are counted in with Mr. Ruther's 'we,' Mr. Gadsden? I asked him, and mother asked him, who 'we' are; but we got very short answers."

He laughed, and said: "You will hardly get more from me. For, indeed, I cannot claim to belong to the 'we' you speak of. I have hardly been a week in town, you know; and almost all this set of men are new to me, for they have come here since I went away. At least I did not know them in those days. But the very first day I came I had to wait in Mr. Ruther's office half an hour for the answer to a despatch he had sent for me, and, while I was there, two of his right-hand men were waiting for him also. There is one of them, — that man who is opening the box of crackers. Well, their talk was about some such thing as this, — it was the baggage of a poor drunken woman that had gone astray, and they were hunting up for her. They could not wait, and I took their message, — glad enough to be of use, — and that seemed to bring me into connection with Mr. Ruther and his 'we.'

"You see," he added, at first in a hurried way, and then more quietly, "if you want to make such a woman as she was live a higher life, — or such a man as your friend John, here, — you must not be harping on one string all the time; and least of all must she herself be that string, or he himself. You must give them somebody else to care for, worse off than they are, or else your pledges, or your resolutions, or what not, are not worth the paper they are written on. But when you get hold of people as affectionate as these Irish people are, it is 'mighty easy' to make them forget themselves, and even to tread under foot their love of whiskey, if you get them fairly excited about somebody else.

"I know it is so, Miss Oelrich," he added more gravely still.

"And I know it is so," said Bertha, " or I ought to know it. And I am much obliged to you for putting it into a formula for me, though I suppose I should have found formulas enough if I had read my New Testament the right way.

"But do you know, Mr. Gadsden, that we talked all this over only on Wednesday?"

"I have a right to ask this time who are 'we'?"

"So you have," and she laughed. "Well, 'we' are my mother and "—

And then Bertha remembered, just too late of course, that the rest of her "we" were exactly the people whom it was hardest to talk of with Will Gadsden. But she was too far in to stop, and, with a face blazing to her hair as she went on, she did go on: "'We' are my mother and Mrs. Claridge, and Dr. Claridge, and Susie and Charlotte."

And by this time she rallied, even under fire, and managed to think that the club plan had been spoken of to somebody beside, and was fairly relieved that to the Claridge family she could add, —

"And Fanny Gregg and Clara Gregg, and I have asked them to speak to their brothers."

Will wanted to relieve her, and, as soon as she gave him a chance, he said, —

"And now it is my turn to be amazed; for, though I have seen Dr. Claridge in most varieties of company, I never thought of him before as going into partnership with the Greggs. He will find the boys are good fellows, too!"

Then Bertha explained, gaining her self-possession as she went on, just what had passed, and what had not passed, in the talks her mother had had with Mr. Ruther and with Aunt Lois, and what she had said to the Greggs, and what she hoped they would say to their brothers. Of course Gadsden was interested: they sat together, talking earnestly, at the end of a settee, while Mr. Oelrich talked politics with the Superintendent of the railroad, and in a moment Will Gadsden beckoned Mr. Ruther to join them. "This man," said he, "knows more and better what we should do than we should find out in six months of blunders." George Ruther disclaimed the compliment, but came eagerly into the talk; and many was the scheme, possible and impossible, plausible and absurd, which these three young people threw out in the rapid mutual interruptions of that eager half hour.

So was it that, all unexpectedly, Bertha Oelrich enlisted two powerful coadjutors in her mother's plan.

But, as I intimated at the end of the last chapter, Satan, or Belial, or Beelzebub, had other plans in view.

Mr. Henry Kingsley has well said that, when the devil cannot find a knave to do his bidding, he sends a fool; and that for many of his purposes a fool answers as well as a knave.

There is a melancholy truth in this remark, although it must not be pressed too far.

Horace and Frank Gregg carefully talked over the "great project," as Horace called it, in memory of the great project of Sully and King Henry, which, alas! came to nothing. Frank had figured upon it, and Horace studied upon it in inquiries too great for figures. Each of them was quite willing to have Mrs. Oelrich bring in her plans, and each of them had suggestions to make to her, both of them glad, if they could, to carry on the Deritend without "perpendicular drinking," when their father came home from a visit, which he called a visit on business to Pittsburg. This visit had retained him there four or five days.

Mr. Gregg, the father, is the fool of whom I have spoken.

The young men had, of course, meant to open to him the new plan as soon as it was in any way ripe. But they were only too well used to carrying on the whole concern themselves, without his lifting one straw's weight of responsibility, and, naturally enough, they had not expected from him any serious opposition as to any suggestion which they might have to make, so they only made sure a regular income for the house, which, in truth, was more than the house had ever had.

Horace said to him at breakfast-time, the day after he returned, that he hoped he would not go out till they had had a chance to talk. The place of Mr. Gregg at meal-times was to preside at the head of the first table, while Horace was in the pantry overseeing the carving, and Frank in the office downstairs.

"No!" said Mr. Gregg. "I have some good news for you!"

When, after breakfast, the father and son met in the little room behind the bar that still bore the sign of "Private Office," which had been painted there in the days of the Deritend's grandeur, Horace was not a little curious as to what this "good news" might be. His father was himself a little afraid of it, he hesitated about bringing it out, and indeed asked Horace first what he wanted to say to him.

Horace, trying to be brief, but becoming quite interested, and talking more than he meant, explained the plan of bringing a wholly new revenue to the house by the institution of a "Deritend club" for gentlemen and ladies.

Mr. Gregg heard without much interest, evidently had something else on his mind, hardly asked a question indeed; but, when Horace had done, he said,—

"Yes, that is all very well, except this tomfoolery about giving up the bar. If they want good club-rooms, they will have to come to us. There is nobody else in town that they can go to, and we can make very good terms with them, I dare say.

"Now, what I have to tell you is much more definite, and it takes no combinations of men and women, to put five hundred dollars' wholly new profits to our bank account, before three weeks are over!"

And then he explained to Horace, half aghast at the explanation, that he had stumbled by the greatest luck on a man named Ferry, at Pittsburg, who was the assignee of a bankrupt liquor-house there, and had, at that moment, to close off without a day's delay all the residue of the table wines of this concern. There were thirty dozen of Champagne, a few boxes of Golden Sherry, ten or twelve broken boxes of Claret, all of good enough quality for hotel use, and beside these some fancy wines, " Green Seal," " Comet-brand," "Cabinet, 1862," and I know not what else, such as never were in the Deritend from the day it was built. "Why, Horace," said the poor old man, in his excitement, "he gave me here the original valuation of the stock, as Wyegate & Foss bought it, — copied from the original invoices. If they were not cheated, — and nobody ever cheated them, — this very wine cost them, — see here, it cost them one thousand four hundred and twenty-three dollars. And, Horace, he offered it all to me, if I would close for the whole of it, for one half the amount on that paper."

If Horace were half-aghast when his father began, he was quite aghast now. But he contained himself.

"That would be a bargain, indeed," said he, "for any one who wanted to make it. But, for us here, I would almost offer those terms to anybody who would take our higher grade wines off our hands. They were what broke Cookman, and I think Gladstone before him here. Why, we do not use in this house ten dollars' worth of first grade sherry or Madeira in three months, and there has not been two dozen of champagne opened here in the last year!"

"No, there has not been," said his father eagerly, "but there must be! This club of yours must do it. I have been thinking of that all day yesterday, that when we had something we could really recommend we should get such people as

Gustav Oelrich and Verspanner and the Thorps and the Stevenses in here. If you want to keep a first-class house, you must have first-class preparations, Horace!"

"Yes, father, if you can. But we cannot. Why, I find it hard to pay for oats and hay the horses use in the stables, and where I am to get another coach, when the great Alleghanian line opens, I am sure I do not know. We must be satisfied, for a while yet, with earning to-day what we spend to-morrow."

He said this as respectfully as he could, for he saw the mood his father was in, and he did not want to cross him. But he was wholly too late. Mr. Gregg brought down his hand with a blow on the table, and said with an oath, —

"We won't be satisfied, my boy, with any such nonsense! We will have a decent house here yet, and something fit to put before decent men. And what I had to tell you was, that I was too much for this cunning Ferry, shrewd as he thought himself. I told him, says I, just what you say to me, — says I, 'There's no demand for high-class wines in Bromwich, and I've got no seven hundred dollars to give you,' says I. And says he,—he'd been drinking a little more than he knew himself,—and says he, 'What's a hundred dollars or so to part friends?' says he, 'name your own price, Gregg,' says he. And says I, 'Ferry,' says I, 'if you'll pack all the wine yourself,' says I, 'and pay the freight,' says I, 'why, I'll give you five hundred dollars for the lot,' says I,—'and I won't give you a damned cent more,' says I. And, Horace, do you think the fool was so hard up that he took me up. He agreed right off to the bargain. He had the wine boxed on Tuesday, and it'll be here by the freight to-night. That's what I waited for!"

"Be here!" said poor Horace, almost screaming. "You have not paid for it! How did he ever let it go without the money?"

"Haven't I paid for it?" said his father, severely. "You don't know how good our credit is then! I have given him the note of the concern payable in thirty days, and he took that for cash. Didn't ask me to add one cent to the face of the note, because I had not the money by me."

Poor Horace, indeed! It was too late to say to his father that they would no more have the money by them in a month than to-day. His father never had understood that "debt" was one of the two devils who consume modern society. Horace himself, perhaps, did not yet understand that "drink" is the other. To have persuaded anybody anywhere to intrust to their keeping any thing of any value, in exchange for a piece of paper, was to this shiftless creature a victory. And Horace and Frank had to make good many a blunder, which by this delusion of his was created.

"Now," said he, fairly rubbing his hands with satisfaction, and wholly unconscious of the weight of what Horace had said, "what you must do — and Frank, and I too, — I shall not hold back — is to get two or three nice parties together here. The Farmers' Club must come, and the college boys must come, and we must blow well about our new stock. It must all be landed here in the day-time, Grosbeck must give you a puff in the 'Eagle' on Saturday, and, Horace, we'll have your money in the bank by the sale of this very

AT THE BOTTOM.

champagne. Don't you trouble yourself about the note! I'll see to that myself, my dear boy."

See to it himself! As if he had seen to any thing but the wretchedness and improvidence of his family since the day he was married to poor Charlotte Sturtevant, and this ill-fated family began!

Horace was in despair. He went and found Frank, and they closeted themselves together. To cut loose from the whole thing, to go to Melbourne or to Yokohama together, would be a blessing. But it was too late for that. They were in the firm, and they could not so easily get out of it. Besides, here were the girls and their mother and the little Fred. No: this was the worst misery their father had lately brought on them. For lately they had kept him to his place as figure-head, and he had shown no disposition to take other place; glad enough, indeed, to have nothing to do, and to have no one goading him to do any thing. But this new freak, bad enough in itself, showed to both of them the danger they were in, in mere matters of money.

Then, for self-respect, for decency! Oh, after what had passed with Mrs. Claridge, after the message they had sent to Mrs. Oelrich, that they should seem to be defying the whole town by this outrageous purchase of wines which everybody knew they could not use, unless they wholly changed the house from what it was even now, — all this was madness!

"Worst of all," said Frank, "that we are expected to decoy Freshmen and Sophomores down here to drink stuff that even old Wyegate could not put off on his customers. I never expected to be asked to do as low work as that is. And then to have that dirty Grosbeck puff us for enterprise in his lying 'Eagle'! Oh, Horace, Horace! how have I deserved to be disgraced so!"

The dirty Grosbeck and the lying "Eagle" did their part of the work only too well. Mr. Gregg sent round his compliments to Mr. Grosbeck, — with a bottle of the new champagne, one of the claret, and one of the "Green Seal," — and his hope that he would call and see the addition that had been made to the Deritend stores at noon on Saturday. And in its "issue" of Saturday the "Eagle" announced that —

"Our excellent friends of the Deritend seem to 'bate no bit of courage as they watch the surging of the great Temperance wave. Eager to meet the demands of an intelligent community, they have given orders in advance to their agents in the great commercial cities, and have been fortunate enough to secure in New York, at the private sale of a connoisseur, a consignment of choice wines fit for an emperor's table. We speak from the *best authority*, 'crede experto,' when we say that no such wines as were received from New York by the Central Railroad on Thursday, at the Deritend, ever before crossed the Alleghany Mountains!

"This is the fit response which these young gentlemen, and mine host, their worthy father, make to the impudent message of the Women's Conference. Had not the ladies better try again?"

And as Mrs. Oelrich read this in the "Eagle" on Saturday, and as Susie showed it to her mother, it was the first answer either of them had to the overtures which Bertha had been told she might address to Fanny Gregg, for Fanny to communicate to her brothers.

Poor Aunt Lois! I remember she laid down the paper with a sigh.

"I had thought better of those young men," said she.

CHAPTER VI.

CAN WE, AND HOW?

WILL GADSDEN had read the "Eagle" of Saturday before Mrs. Oelrich, and before Aunt Lois.

Will Gadsden had seen the triumphal reception of the boxes of wine on Thursday. He had seen the delight of the bar-tender, the fatuous self-gratulation of Mr. Gregg, the jolly sympathy of all the negro waiters, who would have sympathized equally with any thing which made excitement, had it been Father Mathew delivering an address on the doorstep, or had it been the broaching of a cask of whiskey.

Will Gadsden had also observed that Horace Gregg had, with very unusual parade, driven off to buy some oats, hours before the wine arrived, as soon as breakfast was over, announcing that he should not be back till night; and that Frank, with equal noise, and attracting all the observation possible, had taken the morning train to

Toledo, and would not return till Sunday morning. Will was a good deal interested, and not displeased to see that the young men took themselves out of the way.

After what Bertha Oelrich had told him, and what he knew she had said to Fanny Gregg, he felt determined to learn, if a man could learn without impertinence, what all this meant, and if Mr. Grosbeck of the "Eagle" was right in saying that here was an answer of defiance to poor Aunt Lois's visit, of which of course the village had been informed, with more or less explanations, within the day after it had been made. Will, also, thought better of the young men than to believe that the parade was of their making. They had put themselves intentionally out of the way yesterday, and it seemed doubtful if they would be more communicative to-day. Will knew, or thought he knew, that Fanny Gregg would die before she would speak of the matter. He also knew, or thought he knew, that Clara Gregg, if he fell into talk with her, would, before she knew it, come out with the whole train of the family politics, and that he should know in fifteen minutes where the sinews of war had been found, — who had conceived this bold reply to the ladies, who had voted for it in family conclave, and who against it; that he should know, indeed, all there was to be known. Will Gadsden was not perfection, as the reader knows, though he was so handsome. And he was sorely tempted for a moment to ask Clara Gregg if she would not like to drive to the Glen with him that afternoon, — quite certain, first, that she would gladly go; and, second, that he should know all there was to be known before they returned. But Will, if frail, was a gentleman: so he dismissed the thought of cross-questioning Clara as soon as it rose; looked again for Horace, — looked in vain; and then sought George Ruther, his better self, to tell him that he was tempted to sound Frank Gregg and Horace, and to ask him if it would do more harm than good. He actually passed Fanny Gregg in the doorway. She was going out also, as if for some shopping; and, as Will passed her, he confessed to himself that, if it had been the pretty, gentle Clara, rather than the tall, handsome beauty, he should have considered this too good a chance to be lost, and have reconsidered his resolution. But it was not Clara, and he hurried on. As he turned the corner of the street, he could not but notice that Bernard Claridge had joined Miss Fanny. Very well: what was more natural?

"I am a fool," said Will Gadsden to himself, "and I make a mystery of every thing I think upon."

As this passed through his mind, he stopped for a moment at the bookstore, to order his "Galaxy," and to enter his name as a candidate for the Book Club; and there, as it chanced, he met Bertha Oelrich again. Her father's carriage, with John Corkery's successor, was waiting for her at the side door.

Will Gadsden did not notice Bertha, but she did notice him at the moment he came in. And then as he turned to go out, with a frankness which I think did her infinite credit, though it is not advised in the "Young Lady's Companion," this "nice," wide-awake girl bravely crossed the shop, and called him before he fairly stepped into the street again.

"Really, I beg your pardon, Mr. Gadsden, but I know my mother wants to know something that only you can tell."

Of course Will said he was at her service or her mother's.

Bertha saw that she had unwittingly called the attention of two or three college boys who were turning over the new books in the little shop, and of the attentive clerks as well. She certainly did not wish to discuss the Deritend Club in their hearing, far less did she want to take Will Gadsden into a corner, as if there were any mystery. Will had tact enough to help her, had he known what her purpose was; but how can you help any one, till you know what she wants to do?

But Bertha solved her own difficulties.

"The lilac, if you please, Mr. Catlin, — the chocolate, and the lavender; but not the pink, nor the salmon color. Will you please see to the envelopes yourself? At eleven o'clock? Then Conrad here will call when he comes round for my father. Have you a moment, Mr. Gadsden? Then perhaps you will come into the carriage with me. I will set you down wherever you are going."

Will handed her into the carriage, followed her, and said he was going to Mr. Ruther's office. He laughed, and added, "I should stop on the way at our famous new Reading-room, and see if he is not 'loafing' there."

Bertha gave the proper order, and then said, "I did not want to talk with all those people hearing all I said; but mamma is wretched about the failure of our club.

"Why, she had talked about it by day and by night. She had persuaded herself that she was going to remodel the village society of America."

"I think she was," said Will Gadsden, gravely.

"Then you understand how enthusiastic she grew about it. Why, she said that the married women all fall back from their girlish enthusiasms and accomplishments, because they have no chance, even for a moment, to meet each other, or even to meet the men they knew when they were young. She says, in her club, she should see Dr. Claridge and Professor Brenner and Mr. Warburton and John Faunce, and I do not know who not, whom now she never sees except at a conference meeting on the other side of the church. She says she used to know them all as well as, — as well as I know you, Mr. Gadsden," said Bertha, bravely; "and she says it's a great pity that just because she is married that should all die away.

"She says society, in such a town as this, is all in the hands of the boys and girls; and she implies that we are all fools, and I am sure some of us are," said Bertha, laughing.

"To tell you the truth," said Gadsden, "I have been brooding rather on the other side. Take as fine a fellow as Ruther here. He plays on the piano better than any man I ever heard, — played Mozart and Chopin and Beethoven, and even Wagner, to me last night till the clock struck twelve. Now he will not go to dancing-parties; I certainly cannot expect him to go on a sleigh-ride; he would not shine in a prayer-meeting. Where is such a man as he to meet, let me say, such a woman as your mother, or as Mrs. Claridge, or as Mrs. Faunce? Of course he can make evening calls. But you know what that means."

"That's just what mother says. She says if he came in to read his 'Spectator,' just as she looked in to see if the 'Atlantic' had come, she should know he was at leisure, and he should know she was.

"Now, is it not too bad to think that all these grand plans are to be broken by the hatefulness of those spiteful Greggs? I did not think anybody could bear such malice."

"My dear Miss Oelrich, pray give them the benefit of a doubt!" cried Will, eagerly. And then she saw that his eager, handsome face grew grave, as he touched his hat, almost solemnly, to some one whom they drove by. Bertha turned as quickly as was decent, but only guessed that it was Susie Claridge who had such power to change her companion's expression. Will Gadsden tried to rally, but in fact forgot what he was talking about, and could only say, —

"I am going to Mr. Ruther, and, as I said, I think it is as likely as not that he will be at the new Reading-room." Then he remembered that he was going to talk with him about the Greggs, and to ask whether it would be quite impossible to enlist the younger men in some Union of the young men of the town, in which women might join with self-respect and decency. But he fell again into one of his eulogies on George Ruther, and what he was, and what he could do.

Bertha Oelrich all this time was wondering how she could manage to overtake Susie, and tell her how it happened that she was carrying Will Gadsden down the main street at ten o'clock in the morning. Even she hesitated as to whether she should dare speak Will's name to Susie.

Mr. Ruther was at the news-room, or on the threshold, and came forward most heartily to welcome Miss Oelrich, and gave his hand to Will as he stepped from the carriage. I need not say that John Corkery recognized the horses, but the poor fellow did not dare appear till he heard Bertha call him, and Mr. Ruther knocked on the window.

"We had a very pleasant evening, John, and mamma will come the next club evening. And, John, Walter wants you to order Frank Leslie's

'Boys' and Girls'' magazine for him, and he will stop himself and pay you."

John Corkery was twice the man for being publicly recognized thus, in his new vocation.

As he went back to the shop, George Ruther said, "I was going to see your father, Miss Bertha; but, if you have a minute, you will do quite as well. May I stop you so long?"

"May you not, indeed?" said she, and she swung her locket. "You may, unless you want me to look down, to look in, and to look backwards."

"Not that, I am sure," said he, laughing. "Yet I want you to carry a message, such as I think you never carried before.

"I do not know in the least what Mr. Oelrich's theory of the liquor laws is, nor do I care. Every man has his own. But I feel sure that he will agree with us that on any theory fifty-one open bars are too many for Bromwich. The college men feel it an insult; our railroad men find it an insult; even the respectable dealers, as they like to call themselves, would cut the number down if they could. But it is so convenient for the politicians to have just so many rallying places for voters that I believe if a hundred and fifty men asked for licenses they would all have them granted."

[Our law in this matter, as I ought to say to readers in other States, is a "Local Option" law. That is what they call it in England. Every town decides for itself the question of prohibition or license. Licenses are granted only by the county court, which has cognizance of civil and criminal suits, and is therefore well acquainted with the class of people who apply for and recommend licenses. These cannot be granted except to a limited number, and on the recommendation of twelve responsible voters. No liquor must be sold to minors, intemperate persons, or on Sunday.]

"I wanted to ask your father if he and his foreman, and some of the other gentlemen on the hill, would not appear next week in support of our remonstrance against the licensing of these 'Northern' people again. Their house is bad in every way. They sell liquor to the school-boys in the No. 4 school. I shall have ten witnesses to prove that. They sell all day long on Sunday. Poor John here knows that. And as for selling to drunkards, good heavens! They make night terrible there. I have to pass there three nights in the week after the express has left, and I do not like to tell you, Miss Bertha, of the things that go on there."

Bertha was trembling with sympathy, not to say with rage. She would tell her father all that Mr. Ruther said, and then she asked, "Who do you say awards these licenses, — prizes for good behavior, I suppose they are?"

"Why, Judge Converse is the sitting judge this term. The applications come before him."

"Mr. Eli Converse, who lives next the Claridges?"

"Of course. He is on this circuit this term."

"Why should not we all go? I was in court once, at the Bearn trial. I think all the ladies would like to go. Would there be any harm?"

"No harm," said George Ruther, gravely. "I should think there might be great good."

And so he bade her good-by. She drove up College Hill to find Susie Claridge, and the young men walked away together.

CHAPTER VII.

CARD-PLAYING AND CHAMPAGNE.

WILL GADSDEN always spent more time than he meant when he joined George Ruther, and occupied himself with forty things which seemed at the moment very necessary, though they were not perhaps quite necessary to a young student of law. But, as Will said, it was Saturday, and there were no lectures, so he might indulge himself a little in the practice, in what the boys at the Medical School would call the Clinique. It was soon dinner-time: he was glad to accept an invitation to dine with Ruther. Then came the pleasant German lesson, which he gave to them all there twice a week; and then Ruther proposed that all hands should take an excursion to the Water-Gap, going out by an accommodation train and returning by an express. A pleasant day for Will, who sighed for society in his attic at the Deritend, and who in his old life at Bromwich had lived in very different fashion.

George Ruther did not expect much help from the young Greggs in what he and Gadsden hoped for, for the younger men of the college and town; but still he did not dissuade Will from sounding them. "I do not see as it can do any harm," he said. "But such people are apt to be on their mettle," said he. "You see we say very hard things of them." So Will went home to the Deritend at ten at night, resolved to find Frank or Horace if he could.

He looked in at the various common rooms, and saw no one. There were one or two travellers in the reading-room, but no one whom he knew. Then he opened the door of a corner parlor, which generally nobody sat in, but which was in no sort private, because he had noticed that it was lighted, and he remembered that he had seen Frank Gregg reading there, of a stormy evening, when nothing was passing.

In a moment he saw that he intruded on the company, and he begged pardon and closed the door. But in an instant it flew open.

"Come back, come back, Mr. Gadsden! No secrets here! no green curtains nor close blinds

CARD-PLAYING AND CHAMPAGNE. 103

in this house, Mr. Gadsden. We show our colors here! Come in, come in,— all friends here! Some old friends of yours. Glad to see you back again. Take a seat, Mr. Gadsden. I've been away ever since you came back! Here's a clean glass, I believe,— good as clean any way. What will you take? Here's to old times, Mr. Gadsden!"

Poor Will was ashamed, and really in terror. All this voluble welcome was from Mr. Gregg, who had not seen him since he left Bromwich, or since, as I said, he was taken away. True, it was ten days, more or less, since Will had taken his lodgings there; ten days which seemed an eternity to him, as it marked an infinite change in his own life. But they were so short that Mr. Gregg's visit to Pittsburg had covered more than half of them. And it was true that, while he welcomed the old Will Gadsden, it was the new Will Gadsden who received the welcome, and received it in presence of six or eight old "friends," so called, all of whom he had met, in old days, at the bar of this very Deritend.

All of them, who could stand, started up to welcome him. Mr. Grosbeck, of the "Eagle," is the only one with whom the reader is, or need be, acquainted.

Will shook hands as cordially as he could, did not take the offered chair, but tried to excuse himself by saying that he was looking for Frank, and had thought he should find him here.

"Frank! oh! Frank! where is Frank! Oh, yes, Frank! He'll be here in a minute, Mr. Gadsden, — take a seat, take a seat, and wait for him. I'll send for him. Frank, — yes, oh, yes! he's just stepped out. Sit down, Mr. Gadsden, and try this Golden Seal, Mr. Gadsden. I'm glad to offer so good a glass of wine as that to so good a judge."

This from Mr. Gregg to poor Will, who had trained himself to regard any drop of wine for him as being sent by some devil from the pit.

"How kind you are, Mr. Gregg! I see you have not changed in three years. You know we always said that you were too good to your guests, and were too hospitable for a landlord.

"I have given up drinking wine. But I will gladly wish 'Prosperity to the Deritend!' Perhaps you do not know that I am living under your roof?"

"Give up drinking wine! Nonsense, boy! You may very well give up what they have been giving you over in the Old Dominion; but you don't find such sherry as this every night. Bring us a clean glass, Sandy,—a clean glass for Mr.— Mr.— Mr. Gadsden. Sit down, Gadsden,—sit down. Frank! yes, Frank, will be here in a minute,—in a minute. Sandy, what are you bothering about there? leave your fiddling, and go find Mr. Frank, and tell him here is a friend who wants to see him."

Poor Will had made his own pit, by being fool enough to give a reason where none was necessary. And he was just irresolute enough to sit down in the place which Mr. Gregg had made for him, between his chair and Colonel Somebody's. But Will would not touch either the claret or the glorified sherry. Indeed, Mr. Gregg hardly noticed whether he did or did not. He was in exactly that condition of body or mind in which he doubted whether he could talk coherently, and so was trying experiments all the time by way of

5*

assuring himself and others that he could. And Will would have escaped under cover of those wearisome iterations about Frank and Frank's accidental absence, and of Sandy's bringing Frank, without Mr. Gregg's knowing what he drank or caring. But Mr. Grosbeck was in another physical or mental condition, — that of fight, namely. Having been much complimented by the company on the manner in which he "had given the women fits in the 'Eagle,'" — that subject, indeed, having been largely dwelt upon in the little supper of the evening, which was now drawing to its close, — Mr. Grosbeck wanted to show that his wit was still keen, and his stroke exact, and where he saw a head he meant to hit it. The sight of two full glasses by a guest who drank nothing engaged his attention, and he saw at once that here might be foeman worthy of his steel.

"Prosperity to the Deritend!" he cried: "prosperity to the Deritend! Why don't you drink to your own toast, Mr. Gadsdad? what's a toast for, when you don't drink to it?" Then he turned to the colonel who was at his right, and said,

"These travelled gentlemen see so much Tokay and Johannisberg, and they hob-a-nob with so many kings and emperors, that they can't touch any liquor when they get home. But "— with an an oath or two — " brother Gregg's Golden Seal is good enough for me ! "

"What's that you say?" said Mr. Gregg, — diverted unfortunately from his experiment of saying what he could say coherently, by this sudden onslaught, — " Mr. Gadsden says our wine is not good enough for him ! Mr. Gadsden, let me tell you that Henry Clay himself drank a bottle of that very wine you turn up your nose at, — he drank it the day of the big flood on Allegheny ; and he said he would be damned if it was not the best sherry that ever come out of Proosia, Mr. Gadsden. Isn't Henry Clay sherry good enough for you?" and he pushed back his chair with an air that implied that if Will did not drink the sherry he would wring Will's neck for him.

Will knew he must humor them all, unless he wanted a fight. He knew, first of all, that here was no time to preach temperance to them, nor to offer them any other pearls. Indeed, he had no object really at heart but to get out of the room without having his own head broken, if he could, and without disgracing Mrs. Gregg's husband, if it were possible. With more tact than could have been hoped for, he said, —

"Prince Metternich has no such wine as that, Mr. Gregg. That I know from the man who supplies his own table, whom I saw when I was in Frankfort. If he had, I agree with you, that the man who drinks bad wine, when he can get good, is a fool."

"Very well," cried Mr. Grosbeck, — "very well. Now stand to your own text, Mr. Parson, and drink good wine when you have it. Gentlemen, I propose that Mr. Gaderad's toast be drunk standing. All up! fill up, everybody! prosperity to the Deritend, gentlemen! There! see what I say, gentlemen: this is a spy from the women's camp. He won't drink his own toast. Turn him out, gentlemen!" All this, with expletive oaths, wherever there was an opportunity.

"I should have been glad enough to have been quietly turned out," said Will the next day to George Ruther; "but it was pretty clear that any sacrifice of that sort on my part would have made matters worse. Old Gregg fairly had his hand on my shoulder; but I laughed good-naturedly again, put it off, and said,—

"'Wait till I have told you a story. This Metternich wine that you talk about, this Johannisberg,—sour stuff, I am afraid we should think it, all of us,—is bottled by an agent of this gentleman I tell you of, in whose wine-vaults I spent two afternoons in Frankfort.'

"I had got as far as this, and was wondering how I was to spin out my tale till I could decently slip to the door, when—smash!—we heard a window crash outside; then an agonized yell from a woman; then the sound of a heavy fall, and of some weight crashing terribly down the great stairway. And, of course, all who could now ran instantly into the hall, to know what it was which had happened."

It was at heavy cost that poor Will had been saved. The sight before the company as they rushed into the hall was indeed terrible. The crash, whatever it was, had wrenched off a burner of the hanging hall chandelier, so that the gas was pouring out from the full pipe, and a lurid, smoky wave of fire was blazing up against the plaster. Senseless across the hall, upon the marble floor, lay Mrs. Meiers, one of the boarders, whom Will recognized as a lady to whom he bowed every morning as he saw her at her seat in the breakfast room. One or two people were trying to lift her. On the stairway, motionless also, was her husband, his head just touching the marble of the floor. Evidently he had fallen, as he ran downstairs. A negro waiter was clumsily trying to lift him; and an exasperating crowd of men and women on the stairway above, enlarging at every moment, were screaming and howling, and doing nothing — as indeed how should they? — to help in the catastrophe.

The presence of Mr. Gregg and his two Colonels and Mr. Grosbeck did not do much to restore order. But the presence of Will Gadsden and of Horace Gregg, who emerged at the same moment from what was called "the private office," did. Not without a certain firm violence, but still in wonderfully short time, a cork was put into the broken gas pipe. Half a dozen candles were brought out in the great plated candelabra of the ladies' drawing-room, and lighted after a minute's fuss. Poor Mrs. Meiers was tenderly carried by Will himself and one of the porters into the drawing-room, and Fanny Gregg and her mother took charge of her. Meiers's body was laid decently and reverently, as becomes death, upon the long settle on which the porters were wont to sit in the hall. The colonels and other "guests" of this ill-fated evening were led to the door, unless they found their own way there, and, as the last of them intimated his willingness to stay and help, Frank Gregg said calmly, and very loudly, "The house is closed for the night." And then, as his unwilling guest withdrew, he shoved the great bolt with an emphasis which the bystanders felt. And then to the quiet group of on-lookers who belonged in the house, he said, "Really, you had better leave for your rooms. I have sent for Dr. Etter and Dr. Drummond. With my mother and sisters, and all the girls and the porters, we can do all that is needed. Good-night, all!"

So that, in presence of his firmness, the excited throng dispersed and retired.

CHAPTER VIII.

SEVEN MEN OF HONEST REPORT.

MEIERS, the victim of the Saturday night tragedy at the Deritend, was always supposed to be a German, and by birth he probably was. He was a tradesman in thriving business, carrying on with a good deal of enterprise and skill a shop on the corner of the street, where he sold almost every thing, from a china mug with a child's name on it in gold round to a boot-jack or a drover's whip. The old established storekeepers of the town did not like him or his : they always called him a Jew, and called his shop the Jew shop. And I know the ladies always made some excuse for having gone there, as if the constitution and laws of Bromwich required that they should "trade" at certain other establishments which had been in operation since Bromwich was a cluster of log cabins. But, all the same, they did "trade" there a great deal. He called his shop "The Auction

Store," in very big letters. And he printed shop-bills with the same heading : that was a grandeur that nobody else in town indulged in.

Although Meiers was called a German, he spoke as good English as most of us did; and he led about with him this poor little wife, who was in her dialect and aspect an unmistakable Virginian. She had had, as we learned, a hard time of it before they established themselves at Bromwich. Meiers was kind enough when he was himself, — and he would be himself for months, not to say years, — but then, just as his house was swept and garnished, seven devils worse than ever had lived there before would come raging in, pell-mell, together. That is to say, he would go on a "spree," "bender," "lark," "time," or whatever the vernacular of his region might call it; and then woe to poor Mrs. Meiers and her two little children.

But lately things had been better. Prosperity was good for Meiers, as I have found it to be for most men. His enterprise at Bromwich began by his bringing in some auction goods for sale, and opening a disused shop for them, expecting to fold his wings like the Arabs and be gone in a fortnight to some other Bromwich. But there was a demand for his laces and muslins, the shop could be had for little or no rent, and it all ended in his establishment as a permanent retail trader, with as good a run of custom as any man had in the county. He sent for his wife and children, and took pretty rooms for them at the Deritend. He shaved very little; but for the first time in his life he shaved daily. He took seats in church and voted at elections, which he had never done before. Instead of being a wandering Ishmaelite, he gave bonds to society, and settled down as a person who had a character to maintain.

All this was very happy for poor Mrs. Meiers and her children.

What they did, or how they spent their time, I am sure nobody knew, and I am afraid nobody cared. In the daytime Mrs. Meiers was behind a counter in the shop, and the ladies were always glad to see her there. In the evening, as Fanny Gregg told me, they always had a good deal of company in their room; but never, till this fatal night, had there been any disturbance there.

On Saturday morning, however, Meiers had told his wife that they were to have a euchre-party in the evening, and had told her who he should ask. They were a set of people, some Germans, some Americans, and one or two men from New Orleans, — Frenchmen, she supposed, — who had been with him a good deal lately, and whom she hated. But playing euchre was something which happened so often there that she did not consider the party in the least out of the way. She put on the children's best clothes and her own, bought some new packs of cards, ordered some apples, oranges, and almonds for the evening, and supposed her duty was done.

As indeed it was.

But when her husband came back to the hotel to tea, having closed the store early, he brought with him the two Frenchmen whom she hated; and so soon as tea was over, — long before the guests to whom she was used came in, — as if from very restlessness, poor Meiers made her sit down with him and his two friends, and begin to play. Still they played nothing but euchre; and, although she did not quite understand his excitability, she was only too glad if it would work itself off on the cards. "I played wrong," said the poor woman, — "I played horribly; but that snake of a Le Maire, who was my partner, pretended not to care, though we lost all the time. How could I play, with my husband in such a fever; and all the time the people coming in, and I getting up to welcome them?"

Well, by eight o'clock there were three games going on at three tables, fast and quiet, a little betting, but nothing of account. About nine, the poor little woman made a movement to produce her modest refection, — rang, and nodded to the waiter who answered her bell. But when the simple fruit and water, which was quite the thing in our simple Bromwich customs, appeared, Meiers scowled at her, threw down his cards, wrote an order on the back of the paper in which the last pack was wrapped, and sent it to the office. It was answered in a moment by a tray of glasses, with champagne in ice. Then it was that for the first moment Mrs. Meiers understood that the new purchases of the Deritend had fired the devil who had slept so long, and that her little party was to be a famous wine-party for her husband's grand guests and for the others who had been bidden to meet them.

"Mrs. Odenheimer was the only lady there. She stayed for one rubber after the wine came in, and then she went away, and took her husband away. That broke up one table. I said I was tired and would not play. We had one table in my room, and one in the little room, — Mr. Meiers has that. I sat knitting and talking with Laurence Odenheimer. He stayed. And in there, — oh! they played, and they played. They did not play euchre there, and I did not dare to see what they played. But twice he rang for more wine. At our table, too, Mr. Fish and Mr. Coffin got noisy, and Coffin turned round and asked me to order another bottle.

"Then I could not bear it any longer, I went and looked over Axel's shoulder. I saw that he did not know what he was doing. I bent over and just whispered, 'Axel, Mr. Coffin wants more wine, and I think he had better go.' Do you know, I don't think it was that : I think they were cheating him, or I think he was losing. He did not know — indeed he did not know — what he said or what he did. He threw me off, though I hardly touched him. He threw his cards in Le Maire's face. He turned on me as if I were a tiger, and bade me leave the room. He whirled up his chair as if he would strike Le Maire, and then he turned as if he would strike me !

"And I did leave the room. I did not know what I did; and I flung the door open, I was so frightened, and I ran downstairs. The last I remember is putting my hand on the banister."

Poor creature ! she was flying from her own husband, when he flung the chair after her. It struck the chandelier, and that was perhaps the crash we heard. And then he missed his own footing, and then —

That was all !

All this, of course, came out at the coroner's inquest. Of course it was made public, with every odious detail, in the two weekly papers. The "Eagle" gave but a bungling account of it, strangely mixed up with a good deal of bragging that "we" were present, which bragging, of course, had to be somewhat abated by explanations that "we" knew nothing about the unfortunate calamity, and had nothing whatever to do with it, and had only arrived in time to render the services which were needed by the unfortunate lady. But any reticency on the part of the "Eagle" was fully made up for by the eagerness of the "Republic" to state all details. As soon as they found out in the "Republic" office that Grosbeck had been "drinking at the Deritend when the row happened," there was no danger but the public would get its full quantum of incident, nor any danger for Mr. Grosbeck lest his presence should pass unheeded.

Before the next week was over, there was an execution in poor Meiers's shop, on the suit of Le Maire and Guyon, the two Frenchmen, so called. They produced promises to pay, written in Meiers's hand and signed by him, which were unquestionable. His bank account was drawn low, the estate was pronounced absolutely bankrupt, the books were in helpless confusion, and poor Mrs. Meiers and her children were beggars. The two Frenchmen left their claims in the hands of a miserable skinflint of an attorney we had in Bromwich. Then they went to Toledo, and that was the last we saw of them.

All this tragedy, and the talk which followed it, wrought people up to no ordinary interest, when the day came round for the annual hearing of petitions for licenses. To tell the whole truth, I never knew till that year when licenses were granted, and hardly if they were granted. I only knew that there was a saloon or other liquor-shop in every street in town, except on the hill. But, as George Ruther had told Bertha Oelrich, here were fifty-one people to apply for this privilege this year, and they had to ask in form. Nor would anybody have asked for a fairer man to hear the petitions than Judge Converse. I do not know what he would have liked best. But the county had voted that licenses should be given, so there was no doubt he would give them to the people whom he thought most fit to hold so terrible a responsibility.

Meanwhile the women were everywhere. They

had a general petition, that no open bars might be licensed, and the number of victuallers' and taverners' licenses might be much reduced. Then they had a "ward petition," in which they went into details. They collected evidence regarding every man who asked for a license, and every woman. They had good counsel, and this time they knew what they were at.

Well, there was hardly a publican in Bromwich who could stand these tests.

It seemed as if all of them had sold on Sunday. Many and many a poor mother came in, and some said that this fellow and that had sold whiskey to her boys and to her girls. The evidence was not very formal perhaps, but after one little incident it was not often challenged. That was this:—

"Petition of James Brosnihan, to be licensed as victualler, &c.

"Oyez, oyez! All ye who, &c., &c., &c., come into court!"

Wayland, who held the women's memoranda for this ward, called Ellen Sullivan as a witness that Brosnihan had violated the conditions of his license last year, and had sold liquor on Sunday.

She was a pretty Irish woman, frightened, but completely in earnest; and she told, at no great length, how her own brother, only fifteen years old, came home the very last Sunday evening "roaring tipsy, may it please your honor, — having been drinking at Brosnihan's all day since noon."

"Were you at Brosnihan's yourself, madam?" asked that gentleman's counsel.

"I'm a decent woman, sir. God forbid that I should be seen inside his dirty doors!"

"How do you know, then, that your brother bought his liquor there?"

"Bekase he told me so, again and again, sir; and he never lies."

"May it please the court: the court sees that this is nothing but hearsay and tittle-tattle. I wonder that my brother Wayland takes up your honor's time with such fol-de-rol, which he knows is not testimony."

Wayland did not appear disturbed.

"My brother Fish does not like our testimony.

I see a witness in court who ought to be relied on, certainly, if this petition is to be supported, — Mr. James Brosnihan himself. Will your honor swear him?"

"Certainly," said the judge, — " certainly. Nothing could be fairer, Mr. Fish. Swear James Brosnihan."

The hulking, stupid-looking tavern-keeper, who had come into court, as he had always done on such occasions, and had not sense enough to suspect that he should have been miles away, moved heavily towards the stand. Mr. Fish, his counsel, stepped quickly towards him.

"Oh, no! brother Fish, you need not advise the witness," said the judge, good-naturedly. "When I was at the bar, we used sometimes to advise witnesses a little before they came into court; but the witness must do without advice here. These are not cases on trial. The court is merely acting under direction of the legislature and executive in a *quasi* executive position. All we want is to get at the best men for these services to the State.

"Swear Mr. Brosnihan."

And then it may well be imagined what confessions and contradictions poor Mr. Brosnihan was forced into, under Wayland's sharp cross-examination; Wayland being stimulated and directed by little slips of paper, which Will Gadsden kept poking into his hand. Brother Fish hopped up, two or three times, as "a friend of the court," he said; but, on the whole, he could not help his client much on the other side of the room. And before fifteen minutes were over Brosnihan had said that he did not sell liquor Sunday; that perhaps he might have sold it without remembering it; that, on an effort to recollect, he thought it was quite possible he had sold it; that to travellers, indeed, he was almost sure his clerks had sold it; that, in fact, he remembered selling it to one traveller himself one Sunday afternoon; and, finally, that the only substantial difference between week-days and Sundays at his house was that on Sundays the wooden shutters were up and on week-days they were down.

Then Mr. Brosnihan was released, in an evident perspiration.

And no more hearsay evidence was challenged that day.

The women also broke down badly sometimes. They had relied much too boldly on the wrongs of their own sex. But more than one Bridget Murphy and Clara Ganzhorn, who had been voluble enough and intelligible enough when they had told the stories of their wretchedness to sympathizing women in their own little "tenements," could not be brought to remember a word, or to say any thing, when they were in their best clothes on the stand before the Judge, in presence of Mr. Fish; yes, and of certain husbands who would beat them within an inch of their lives, when they got home, if they were displeased with the drift of their testimony.

Still the field-day ended in a disastrous rout of the publican forces. The women had piled up so much testimony that Wayland and the other young gentlemen who had volunteered as their counsel could well afford to have three-quarters of it break down. "If only," said Wayland, laughing afterwards, "they would have marked on the brief the witnesses that would stick as distinguished from those who were 'very interesting,' but had no backbones." The end of the matter was that there were not, of all the fifty-one petitioners, more than ten who passed with their skirts free through this terrible fire. Some of these possibly deserved their immunity. Thus the Deritend had merely sent in its petition, had no counsel and no representative; and young Revel, who held the women's memoranda for that ward, had not a witness against the Deritend whom he dared call. He was quite sure that plenty of college boys had drunk at that bar, who were under age. But he could only suspect in general, and he knew the court would not let him call witnesses in the least at random. Actually, after all that had been said and written about the Deritend in the last month, in this tournament of tongues, nobody said one word against its fair fame.

"I would as gladly have put old Gregg on the stand, as you did your Mr. Brosnihan," said Revel to Wayland. "But, if he is an old fool, he knows enough to keep away from the court while his petition is read. I wonder if they had any counsel?"

"I think not," said Bernard Claridge, a little

unguardedly. "Frank Gregg said the petition might stand or fall by itself; that if he was not a good citizen, sober and respectable, which is what the law requires, and Judge Converse thought he was not, he should like to know it."

And, as Bernard said this, he colored quite unnecessarily, and walked away from the little group of young lawyers. I wondered why.

You see in such a town as ours all the brightest young fellows at the county bar were in "Society;" and if "Society" chose to reduce the taverns of the village from forty to ten, why "Society" had a very reliable ally in the rising lights of the law.

The Judge took a day to make up his decisions. On Wednesday we all gathered in the court-room again, and the announcement made was fairly dramatic. He said that the evidence which had been volunteered, that there ought not to be any such establishments as he was directed to license, did not seem to him to be pertinent to the occasion, however interesting in itself. He said that his duty was rather functional, or *quasi-*executive; it was one of a class of undefined duties which from the days of the English practice devolved on the circuit courts, or their judges, because then judges were magistrates, supposed to be well known in the community. But it was not a duty of strictly judicial character. Then he read the statute, and said that his duty was clear: he must appoint one sober, intelligent, and discreet person for every ward in Bromwich, who should receive the license of the State for selling liquors as a victualler or taverner, if he gave the requisite bonds. He might appoint more at his discretion. But he had no discretion to refuse to appoint any. It was not necessary for him to appoint people because they asked. But the presumption was in favor of persons who publicly asked, if, after as full canvass of the facts as had evidently been made here, no testimony appeared against them.

After this preface, he said he should appoint one — and but one — victualler to act as taverner in each ward. The duty of selection was not difficult, he said, in most cases. And he read a list of eight persons who had applied for licenses, and against whom, he said, no charges of serious import had been sustained. In the other four wards he had been obliged to select himself. He found that in three of them there were apothecaries who held apothecaries' licenses already. They could not act as taverners; but he should consider the purpose of the law fulfilled, if he gave to them victuallers' licenses.

"As for Ward III.," he said, "I find no name. Mr. Clerk, have you a list, or has any person in Court a list of the storekeepers in Ward III.?"

A reporter of the "Republic" handed to his honor the "Business Directory" of Bromwich, with the page turned down at Ward III.

The truth was that the division of Bromwich into twelve wards was an absurdity, only made that we might have twelve aldermen; and why we had twelve aldermen "no feller could find out."

The Judge looked along the short list of stores and shops.

"There is no apothecary in this ward," said he, "and no grocer. Every saloon in it has been shown to be hopelessly corrupt, and a scandal to the borough. There is only this little gore," he said, "which comes into the trading part of the town.

"Yet I must appoint one discreet, sober and intelligent person here with a victualler's license." And he paused a minute, scanning the book again.

Then he laid it down with some feeling: the court-house was hushed.

"Mr. Clerk, appoint Emeline Meiers, widow of the late Axel Meiers. I understand she continues his business at the same stand. She ought to be discreet in this matter. Send a note to her to say that, if she will give bonds for this business, which the State regards as so necessary, she will be approved by this court."

The people who heard that decision went home to discuss the matter with quite clear light as to what the notions of the Judge were.

"And now we have done with this for a year," said he.

"Mr. Clerk, call the docket."

CHAPTER IX.

WALKING AND TALKING.

THE reduction of the number of our saloons and drinking-places from fifty-one to eight would have been in itself a revolution, had it really happened. But, of course, such things do not come out in fact as they do on paper. We do not have any police in Bromwich, and it would not have made any difference if we had. Still the forty-three suspended people had to conduct their business much more cautiously than they did before. The "Sons of Pythias" swore that they would prosecute every man of them who had a sign up; and, indeed, a good many of them folded their tents, and went to parts unknown. My uncle, Dr. Claridge, said to Aunt Lois that she must not expect much more from the courts or from the law than they had gained. He said that his only object was to keep temptation out of the way of the college boys, of his own sons, and of the young shopkeepers and mechanics who had not contracted a passion for liquor. As for those who had, he said, like John Corkery or like Edward Felton, anybody who loved them must begin at the other end. And, unless somebody loved them, he said there was no help for them.

Anyway, we got quiet Sundays. All influential parties were at one there. The manufacturers did not want any black Mondays, the railroad people didn't want their hands off on sprees, and those "victuallers" and "taverners" who had escaped as by fire did not mean to risk such an ordeal as that in which poor John Brosnihan had gone under. So our Sundays, in these pleasant autumn days, took on almost a foreign air. You would see the German and Irish workmen in their best, with their smart wives and their toddling little ones, scattered along in groups all the way out on the tow-path of the canal. I will not swear but you might have found boys playing base-ball in the afternoon, if you had walked out to the Feeder.

Bertha Oelrich, who was a stout walker, was

walking home one Sunday afternoon after the Sunday school, when, as she passed the Hazards, she met Mr. George Ruther. They were very good friends now, and he said very frankly how glad he was to see her. Then he asked if he might turn and walk with her, if, as he supposed, she were going home.

Bertha invited him cordially to join her, and they walked briskly and gayly on, in full enjoyment of the lovely day.

For the reader is begged to understand that, though little else has been said of any thing in Bromwich but the fortunes of "Our New Crusade," many other things were said and done there all this time. The sun rose and set, smokes curled up in peaceful skies in the morning and intimated that there were griddles, beefsteaks, and coffee below. The corn ripened, and the pumpkins took on the hue of gold. The girls pressed maple-leaves and ferns; and girls and men talked of ten thousand things besides licenses and Sunday sales. It is only that in the history of "Our New Crusade" comparatively little space can be given even to the most important of these things. It might, for instance, be taken for granted by the author that the reader will understand that the sun rose and set, and also that young men walked briskly and gayly, when on matchless Sunday afternoons they found themselves in company with true and brave and beautiful young girls.

So George Ruther walked with Bertha Oelrich, and talked of this and of that: of his residence in Russia; of the winter she spent in Altenberg; of the good English of the Russian gentlemen; of her difficulties in following the German play, of the way in which she learned German over again from her father's relatives, whom she was visiting; of his odd blunders when he tried to talk Russian, and so on. And thus he was led, not unnaturally, to speak of the pleasant Saturday afternoons they had at his house, as Will Gadsden met them for their German lesson there.

"Everybody takes part on Saturday, whatever it is on other days. Even my little Ralph has learned to kiss his 'theuer oheim' with a 'guten abend,' when he goes to bed."

"I really think you ought to enlarge your

class, Mr. Ruther," said Bertha, a little off her guard.

"I tell Gadsden that he is too good a teacher to be wasted. The truth is he was in excellent hands at Halle, and then he has the gift of teaching, and the gift of tongues too.

"Indeed, I know very few gifts he has not," added Ruther, after the longest pause since they had joined each other.

"Mr. Ruther, we are thinking of the same thing. Do you think he has the gift of all gifts, on which every thing depends for him. Do you think he will hold on?"

"God only knows that," said he, reverently. "Indeed, that is what dear Will would say himself. He would say that he could do nothing without help. But I will say that I am absolutely sure of him. I am as sure of him as I am of myself; and I do not know what this temptation is, I cannot conceive of it. No merit of mine; but he was born with this fire in his veins! Oh, dear! how I wish that about the third and fourth generation were not true; but it is horribly true, alas! and he, poor boy, is fighting his grandfather's devils, as perhaps he, poor soul, fought his.

"To go back, I am more sure of him than I am of myself. I look on him as I might look on the figure in Daniel's vision, treading unscathed on coals of fire!"

And the tears fairly stood in his eyes, as he turned to speak to her. Bertha, too, was very much affected, — so much so that she said what she was sorry for a moment after: —

"Do you know I feel the same about her? I told my mother, last night, that I look on her as Dante looked on Beatrice. Why, she was counting stitches in some knitting for me yesterday, and I longed to say to her, 'Susie, you are an angel.' And he never speaks to her, he never even goes there. And she never even breathes his name."

"I thank you a thousand times," said George Ruther, "for being willing to allude to her." And then, with all his own tact and delicacy, he added, "And you shall never regret your confidence. I will not — I hope I need not say I will not — let him dream that you have spoken to me of her. You see I have only guessed; that is, you know I am a stranger here. But I knew, I could see what a noble creature she is; and perhaps I know better than most men could know that he is very worthy of a most noble woman's confidence and love."

"I am so glad you say so," said Bertha, — "so glad. It is a comfort to know and feel this, though, of course, I cannot lift a finger nor say a syllable, though I am the dearest and nearest friend she has; and, indeed, I love her, Mr. Ruther, as never woman loved woman, I believe."

She was half-laughing and half-crying as she spoke. But she turned to him, and smiled bravely upon him through her tears, because she was so proud to be the friend of such a woman as Susie Claridge.

And he, — he was proud to be the friend of such a man as Will Gadsden, and to testify to somebody of what Will was and could be.

Yes; and both of these young people were proud and happy, because they had for once talked of the eternal realities with each other. There are but a few great words, and of those few they had spoken one or two. There are but three realities which never die : they had alluded to them all, in what they had said of Will Gadsden and Susie Claridge, who seemed so fatally parted.

These three realities are, —

FAITH, HOPE, LOVE.

They were written in other language on the faces of Bertha's locket.

They were the inspiration of the four mottoes of George Ruther's "we."

CHAPTER X.

PHI NU.

MEANWHILE Horace Gregg and Frank Gregg had their troubles, although the license granted to the Deritend, per force, had seemed to establish that house quite above the heads of all other institutions of its kind.

Thirty days is long to the school-boy awaiting his vacation. It is long to the lover waiting the wedding-day. But it is very short, alas! to the poor deluded wretch who has put his name to a promise to pay, which is to come due in thirty days. It is shorter yet, when, as in the case of these young men, somebody else who can speak for them has put his name to the note, and they have not had the privileges and immunities, whatever they may be, which the note secures.

Thirty days were grinding by with pitiless rapidity. Hearing of coroners' inquests, hearing of license petitions, Indian summer, every thing else, agreeable and disagreeable, seemed only to hurry forward these hated thirty days.

Yet at the end of these thirty days the note of the firm "Charles Gregg and Sons" must be paid at a Pittsburg bank. And thus far the only poor "asset," which had not been spent within the week in which it came in, was the claim of the firm upon the bankrupt estate of Axel Meiers "for two months' board, self and family," and for several "sundries," conspicuous among which were "eleven bottles Cliquot champagne in own room."

"I wish I did not feel so angry about it," said Horace to Frank one day, as they spoke with each other in the private office. "I cannot bring my mind to it, as I should to an account for flour or oats or hay. Five hundred dollars, more or less, as he says, will not make us or break us. But, if he means ever to get us into such a scrape again, we are broken already."

"You know?" — said Frank, with hesitation. And Horace would not let him finish the question.

"Oh, yes! I know, I know only too well, — it is that which makes me so angry, — that I am expected to stay downstairs here on the night of Thursday, while a hundred and fifty poor boys and their friends get half-fuddled upstairs, and that I am to be praying God that they may take off my hands a hundred and twenty bottles of unsalable wine, so that I may meet my honest debts next morning! It is too bad, and I cannot stand it."

What he meant was that on that Thursday there was to be a great Anniversary of the Phi Nu Society, and the supper had been ordered by the Local Committee at the Deritend House. Whenever Horace warned his father that something must be done about this miserable five hundred dollar note, as well as about forty other claims which hung over the firm, the fatuous man always said, "Oh! after the Phi Nu we shall be in clover," or "After the Phi Nu we can settle every thing." Horace had gone out from the office in disgust a dozen times, because he had heard his father put off one or another butcher or farmer, or even egg-woman, by saying, "If you had as lief wait till the fifteenth. We have some money coming in on the fourteenth, and we can pay you then."

Men of the type of fool to which Mr. Charles Gregg belongs invariably regard a fixed sum of money which is in the future as being applicable to as many purposes at the same time as they may need to use it for. The same six hundred dollars due him would, in any event, be made by Mr. Gregg's imagination to pay ten separate debts of five hundred dollars hanging over him. And thus it was with perfectly good faith that he assured one and another creditor, pressing him for payment of honest dues, that on the fourteenth he should have some money.

Horace and Frank were not fools. They were men of business; and they knew, to a cent, what they had to do, and to an hour when they had to do it. Things were not going well with the Deritend House, but the young men were prudent and sensible. Frank was carrying on his stables with the lowest conceivable expenditure, and he said to Horace that he did not dare tell him how small were the stocks of grain he kept in hand. But for all their prudence and care it was none the less true that luck seemed to go against them. That whole story of Meiers's death had gone into all the papers, and the house had been unfortunately advertised by it far and near. Since that happened, travellers who knew nothing of Bromwich had been very apt to take the " Northern " coach instead of the " Deritend," at the station, when they wished to go to a hotel. So the " transient " receipts fell off. One or two of the most reliable families of " boarders " had made some excuse to leave. And so Frank and Horace knew, more than they had ever known, the difficulty of keeping their expenditures anywhere near a cash level. Meanwhile here was this fussy, shiftless father complicating every thing, and leaving them with all the responsibility, while they had only half the control.

Before this Thursday came, of which he said so much, and from which he hoped so much, he had a dozen opportunities to confound the best plans of the young men, whom he chose always to call the boys, and to overlook, while he rested upon them entirely.

Thus, Frank had been in the habit of buying hay of an old German farmer, who lived in the valley four or five miles above us. The account had run on unadjusted rather longer than Frank liked; but as matters went, as he knew old Otterbein was their friend, he told him frankly that he wanted to buy twenty tons more of hay, but he would rather meet the payment for the whole after Christmas. He proposed what pleased the old man perfectly, to give to him the firm's note, due on the 4th of January, for the whole sum.

The old man was entirely satisfied; came down himself with the last grand procession of his teams, and, when the last blade of hay was delivered, walked round into the house well pleased, to announce that it was there. Perhaps he expected that Horace or Frank would ask him to stop and dine, as indeed they would, had they been there.

Instead of Horace or Frank, he found their father; and, by misfortune, found him in one of his most pompous moods. He was talking grand to a General Wardour who had strayed into the hotel reading-room, and who was expected to be Governor of Iowa or Colorado or Utah, Mr. Gregg hardly knew which.

With company so grand, he could hardly recognize Mr. Otterbein.

But when the good old farmer at last compelled him to be aware of his presence, he said, in his most jaunty and condescending air, —

"O Hans, is it you? Come about some hay? Well, wait a little while, and Frank will see to you.

"I was saying, General, that if the country understood that when gold ranges higher than fifty per cent above the cost of paper"—

"Ef you would dake care of your own gold and your own paper, id would be pedder vor you."

This ejaculation from the indignant hay-master arrested the political economy, and called forth the ill-concealed laughter of all the lazy dogs who were wasting the morning in the reading-room.

Mr. Gregg became more patronizing than ever.

"Well, Hans, what's the matter?" said he, just winking to the General, in a very noticeable aside. "When did you begin to study finance?"

"Mebbe I know wot I say, mebbe I don't know. Here I pe, for my money, or for the note of hand Mr. Frank — that's your poy — promise me."

Mr. Gregg was not usually indisposed to give notes of hand to any one who was fool enough to take them; but he was in the vein of showing off to the General. He knew nothing of Otterbein's account, and knew he knew nothing of it, and, in short, he wanted to get rid of him.

"Don't be a fool, Hans, — don't be a fool! Come for your money any time but now. Don't you see I'm busy? General, step into the parlor with me, and let me open a bottle of our genuine Henry Clay. You don't see such wine every day!" So he actually turned his back on old Otterbein, who, though he was in overalls and smock, expected, with some reason, to be treated with some consideration.

The idlers in the reading-room watched the scene, and snickered aloud.

This did not improve the old man's temper. "Mebbe he's too good for me to talk to. I'm not too good to pring hay to his parn, nor oats to his horses. Tam fool! I could puy him and sell him, and I suppose I petter pegin!"

It was true enough that the comfortable old fellow could have bought and sold the Deritend House, ten times over, had he chosen. And he was the man whom Mr. Gregg had chosen to insult in company.

He crossed to the county bank in a rage, and went up to the cashier, who was always very friendly to him.

"Tell me some goot lawyer, Mr. Newland, some man tat will not cheat me. This blackguard Gregg will pay me no money, and laughs when I ask him."

Mr. Newland really tried to soothe him, but without avail. The old man did not make his story very clear, but Newland knew him well enough to know that the foundation must be sure. He must have dunned Gregg for money, that Gregg could not or would not pay. And Otterbein was very patient with people who owed him. Mr. Newland had to name a lawyer, and the old man left him, vowing that he would have an officer in the house before the week was over.

Now it was at this same county bank that within half an hour Horace had offered for discount the note of Gregg & Sons, knowing, that by some such relief he must be prepared to meet his father's rash obligation at Pittsburg. The cashier meant to discount the note, though he did not fancy it much, but he really wanted to oblige. The president would be in the next day, and he would let Horace know.

This was the man to whom at this moment was brought the intelligence that the Deritend could not pay an honest bill for hay, and insulted such a man as Hans Otterbein.

When Horace came in the next day for his money, Mr. Newland told him that he found they had passed their line of discounts, that the president was very firm, and that he could not discount his note.

This is the sort of mischief which can be done by a fool.

"Who cares for old Hans?" said the befooled Mr. Gregg on Thursday morning, in the midst of the preparation for the great Phi Nu supper. An intimation had come in that, unless immediate payment of his account was made, an officer would be placed in the house the next day. "Who cares for old Hans? Why, we shall net from this very supper more than the whole amount of his dirty bill!"

This boast was addressed to Frank, who knew only too well what this extra game and confectionery was costing; how much he was to pay for the servants he was obliged to hire for this feast, and who at that moment was beside himself for current money to meet even its accidental expenses. He knew also why Horace did not hear the speech. It was because Horace was here and there and everywhere, trying to rake together what must be brought together for the payment, absolutely essential, of the next day, when his father's fatal wine-note must be provided for at Pittsburg.

"Your wine-money is always cash down," continued the prating father, perfectly conscious of the cause of Frank's uneasiness. "Not a man of them leaves this house to-night without settling for his little wine card. There's five or six hundred good dollars for you, alone, Master Francis. No waiting for your bill to be audited, or such nonsense."

"Ferguson has not made me wait much for to-night's bill," said Frank, sadly. "He has paid me very handsomely on account, already. I don't know where his supper would be, had he failed to." Then he paused, before he said, "Are you really hoping that these boys are going to order two hundred bottles of champagne? There will not be a hundred and sixty of them here."

"Oh, don't be critical, Frank! What's a dozen more or less? I mean we shall all be in clover to-morrow morning!"

The Phi Nu was a literary society with branches in forty or fifty colleges in the Middle, Western, and Southern States. The conventions were held in turn at different colleges, and were occasions of great interest among college students and their friends. This year it came to Bromwich for the first time. The "Local Committee" of our own Bromwich College was on tenter-hooks of anxiety, lest the reception and entertainment should not be equal to that which the convention had received at Lexington, at Charlottesville, at the Ohio Oxford and the Ohio Athens. We had the

Mozart Band from Philadelphia, for the music, at a fabulous expense. And Ferguson had, in truth, met Horace and Frank Gregg more than half way, and had provided for the supper so generously that they might re-enforce the Deritend where it was weak, and be able to meet the tastes of delegates who knew personally of the elegancies of entertainment of the St. Charles at New Orleans, and the St. Nicholas, which was then famous, in New York.

And the young men were happy in what our Local Committee did not arrange, — the choice of orator and poet. I was tempted to call the orator "Fisher Ames," that I might rightly give an impression of the reputation he brought with him, though that was not, and is not, his name. His name was and is Benjamin Brannan, and at the time of our story he was just earning a reputation among all thoughtful young men for ripe and pure oratory. It is now years since that Brannan with his nearest friends left this world together. For poet, we had William Ramsdell, just then ordained. Long since he has given up the writing of verses, in the more attractive work of the writing of sermons. But I have never known one audience laugh and weep as did our audience that night as he read his poem.

But it is not my business to report the poem or the oration. A long procession filled and overfilled the church. The music was exquisite; the oration was a noble appeal to a body of fine young men, and it almost brought them to their feet, once and again, in the ecstasy of their enthusiasm and applause. Of the poem I have spoken. Then a song sung by the Phi Nu delegates, and then a procession to the Deritend.

I am not a Phi Nu myself. But by a great favor, because Ramsdell was staying at Dr. Claridge's house, I was squeezed in at the supper, with many vows of secrecy, if I should there learn any of the secrets of the order. Be at ease, secretaries and ex-secretaries, for I learned not one. There were fully a hundred and fifty young men there, — half of them from our college, half of them delegates. They were jolly, not noisy; but now and then some capital joke, at one or another point of the horseshoe tables, brought out a scream and shout of laughter which, for the moment, drowned all talk. Then we would all begin again.

The president of the evening was a Philadelphia millionnaire, who remembered Bromwich and Phi Nu, and had been well pleased to knit together again his remembrances of his college days. At his right hand was Ramsdell, at his left was Brannan, and Ferguson next to him. I sat near enough to Ferguson to hear all these magnates said.

So soon as we had finished our game, Mr. Charles Gregg himself, with quite a flourish, handed to the president an elegant wine-card, which had been printed for the occasion, with the monogram of Phi Nu at the top. Similar cards had been passed all down the table.

Mr. Wister handed it to Brannan, and asked him what he should order. "Let my order go for us all three," he said, with a smile.

Brannan paused a moment, seemed to think he must speak quickly, if he spoke at all, and then said, "Really, Mr. Wister, I do not usually drink wine after ten o'clock at night. I am sure these boys do not, or ought not, if they do. Now they will want to do what gentlemen older than themselves do, and they will be very much governed by what you and I do. I do not care for doing good for example's sake. But I should certainly rather set the example of the habit of my life at home."

"God bless you, my dear fellow," said the impetuous man, "you're wholly right. Why did I not see this myself?" And he sprang to his feet.

"Brethren of Phi Nu! I propose our first toast a little early, — 'Eternity to Phi Nu!' And I wish to make a proposal.

"I propose that we drink it in cold water. I shall, and I hope you will. I do not say I am a teetotaller; but I do say that I was one when I was in good old Bromwich, — God bless her! — and that, if I had not been, I should not be here to-night. I do not want to have Dr. Witherspoon miss a man of us from morning prayers.

"Now every man is free here to order any wine he chooses, and I see some excellent wines named on the bill; but I want Phi Nu's health drunk in water. And I just propose that we drink all the toasts that follow in the same way!"

He certainly surprised his audience. But he did not speak to an unsympathizing crowd. Phi Nu always had the best scholars in the colleges, men who knew it was best to keep their heads cool. Our own representation was of men and boys who drank very little, if any thing, beside water. Still no one had wanted to seem mean to guests from a distance; and the guests from a distance did not want to seem mean to their hosts. And I know, for one, that I should have ordered my bottle of champagne or of sherry, simply that Bromwich might give as elegant an entertainment as Cleveland gave last year.

But here was Mr. Wister — a man who could buy wine in all the markets of the world, if he chose, — a man who had bridged the Youghehagany, and had sent fleets to the Antipodes — coolly intimating that he thought it was rather the best breeding not to take any wine at all!

The courage of the proposal pleased some men. The proposal itself pleased others. Tom Davis hopped up, and said, "Amen! three cheers for the president," — which were given.

And then they drank "Eternity to Phi Nu" in

water, and there was not a drop of wine opened at that supper party that evening. I am not sure but the fashion was set for Phi Nu to the present day.

And by such a misfortune ended Mr. Gregg's well-founded hopes of paying for his wine purchase by the Phi Nu's supper!

CHAPTER XI.

WORD TO PITTSBURG.

"WHATEVER else happens, Horace, you must and shall go to bed."

This was what Frank said to Horace after the last of the young fellows had gone home at three o'clock Friday morning.

"Go to bed with a note protested at Pittsburg before sundown! Much good will the bed do to me!"

This was Horace's reply.

Their father had taken his candle to go to bed hours before.

But Frank had his way. Somehow, Frank always did have his way with Horace. And at four o'clock in the morning silence reigned over the Deritend.

But at five the early passengers were called. At half-past five the early breakfasts were ready. At half-past six the gong rang. At seven the regular breakfast began to be served to all comers till ten, just as if the house had not been in an uproar the night before, and just as if that fated note were not going to protest at Pittsburg, for all Horace's skill to prevent it.

And every one was at his place or her place, — Mrs. Gregg at the ladies' table, Horace in the office, Frank in the store-room, — just as if disgrace were not immediate and ruin impending.

Fanny Gregg was perhaps a minute earlier than her wont at breakfast. Bernard and I had spent what was left of the night at the hotel, that we might not disturb the Doctor's household. As we passed her to our seats at breakfast, we both bowed; and she bowed, and tried to smile. But clearly it was an effort. Her face was intolerably sad.

Bernard said very little; did not choose to go back over the Phi Nu supper, as Gadsden, who was sitting by us, tried to make him; and the moment Miss Fanny left the table, which she did in a few minutes, Bernard went after her, leaving his breakfast untouched, for it had only just been brought, in answer to his order.

"What is that?" said I to Gadsden, fairly surprised. "Does he know her as well as that?"

"He is very often here," said Will, "and I have often seen them together. Any man might be proud of knowing as noble a girl as that is. This house," continued Will, "is a problem to me. It seems to me hell, sometimes, when I think of what I have seen in the bar-room here, or of that wretched Mrs. Meiers's suffering. But when I see the loyalty of those two girls to their mother and their brothers,— nay, when I see the way Horace and Frank, as we all call them, carry each other's weights — it seems to me a part of the kingdom of heaven.

"They do have a hard row to hoe, — to make a place decent and respectable, which stands on the foundation of that room downstairs.

"I never look at Horace Gregg," he added in a minute, "without thinking of Hamlet. The world is out of joint for poor Horace, and it is a cursed spite that so fine a fellow as he should be out of his place in righting it."

"How well they both behaved last evening!"

"Did not they? Gentlemen through the whole,

not above their business, not a hair's breadth below it. If they had any weight to carry, one did not see it."

"Yet where that fool, their father, is, there must be weights to carry."

At this moment Bernard Claridge came running back. "Fellows, come here," he said, — "come into the office with me."

The private office was an inner mystery to me. I had passed its door often, but never entered it before. We hurried across the dining-room with Bernard, as he begged us. In the private office we found Horace and Frank.

"It is worse than I said, Claridge," said Horace, sadly. "I told you that there were four fifties in the safe. There were last night in this pocket-book. To-day the pocket-book is empty!"

This he had discovered, while Bernard was crossing the dining-room.

"In short," said Bernard, eagerly, "this firm has a note of five hundred dollars, to be paid this day at the First National. To pay it with, they had these two hundred dollars, and these are gone!"

"Is it Garnet?" asked Gadsden. Garnet was the office clerk.

"I wish I did not think so. I have sent to his room."

"Mr. Garnet is in bed, sare. But he will be down instantly."

"Then it is not Garnet. It is — it must be — Oh, my God! it must be my father!"

A father stealing from himself, and from his own sons!

Frank had run out of the office, had found his mother, and with her went to his father's bedroom.

While we were all yet excited and confused, he returned, his face white as death, and his eyes swimming with tears.

He whispered to Horace, while we three looked at the "Eagle," at the framed diploma on the wall, or out of the window.

Then there was a dead silence.

"It is too true," said Horace then, and he said it very sadly. "After he found last night that — that — that he should not sell his wine, this poor man — took this — took these wretched bills across to Norris's, — you know, I suppose, they play there every night, — and he played, and he played, till it was all gone!

"I cannot ask you to feel sorry for him, fellows; but I do, indeed I do."

Then for a minute no one said any thing more.

For me, I was wondering how we all came to be there; why this proud Horace, usually so reserved, had asked us all three into this private office, to a story of family shame; or, indeed, what was the story we had been called to hear? For this loss of the money was as much a surprise to my cousin Bernard as to me.

Bernard undertook to explain. Will, with his head as clear as always, helped every thing forward by one or two bold inductive conjectures.

The truth was that Bernard had followed Fanny, and had insisted on speaking to her. She was in tears, as he thought she was. And — though Bernard did not tell us this then, we knew it afterward — Fanny trusted him, and believed him, yes, and began to wish she might rest on him, as one day she would have said she could only rest on Horace. And Bernard had soothed her, poor girl, and had sympathized with her, as she sat by him in the ladies' parlor, till at last she could keep her secret no longer, and she had told him that Horace was beside himself because that day they should be disgraced. The firm's note would go to protest, he had told her, and they would all be bankrupt to-morrow.

Not all of this, but enough of it, Bernard told to us in the private office.

"It is hard," said poor Horace, "after the fight we have made for it, to have it all come to an end so suddenly and so soon. And I cannot help saying still, that the cause is very small!"

Then the poor fellow turned away, as if he were resolved that he would not break down, and that nothing should make him shed a tear.

"We ought to say, however," said Frank Gregg, "that it is not this one note alone. Every thing is against us. Old Mr. Otterbein, whom I thought our friend, swears he will have an officer in the house to-morrow. That will frighten away boarders, the transient company has stopped already. Our quarter's rent is due on the first. That is the heaviest single bill we pay. Taxes, as you all know, must be paid before December. And, indeed, you know how many forgotten claims appear the moment there is a screw loose anywhere."

"But I called you two in," cried Bernard, eagerly, "that there need not be a screw loose anywhere. I don't see that this thing need go beyond us five in this room. I have two hundred and twenty-three dollars, which may go to Pittsburg as soon as the telegraph can take it. Just now he had two hundred more in that pocket-book," this the poor fellow said with a sorry face, "and I knew you two would go seventy-seven if you could. That's what I called you for."

"Of course we would," said Will, "I can go more than that. I have one hundred and eleven dollars in the bank now. Horace, I'll pay you twenty-two weeks' board in advance," and he laughed. Horace did not laugh. No, his eyes did fill with tears, after all. For Gadsden had never called him "Horace," — no, not for near three years, not since the old black times!

For me, I could offer nothing. The term was nearly ended, and I had not five dollars in the world. At that time in my life, indeed, I had never but once had thirty dollars I could call my own.

Will Gadsden was writing on a card. In his quick way he poked his head out of a little slide. "Sam, go saddle the white mare. Take this card to Mr. George Ruther. Tell him to ride her back, and come afoot yourself."

"I beg your pardon," said he to Frank, laughing again, "for anticipating your orders. But Ruther will understand that this is a time, if any, to 'Lend a hand.'"

Ruther did understand it. He was with us in ten minutes. Before an hour was over, four of us were in separate wagons from the stable, and the other two out on foot. We were carrying out the necessary details of a quick morning's work, in which each man of the six was bearing his brother's burthens. I, of all people in the world, was sent out to Hans Otterbein. I talked to him, explained to him, soothed him, and ended in persuading him to take the boys' note of hand, assuring him that the father should leave the firm before midnight. George Ruther waited on Mr. Newland at the County Bank, put his own name on the back of the faulty note; and then it proved that, although the discount line was overstepped, it could be, just for once, overstepped a little more. Bernard went up to see Ferguson, — who was entirely reliable, — and came back at noon with two hundred and ten dollars, the balance of the supper account, which Horace would have died before he would dun for. Frank was closeted with Wayland, drawing up an instrument, by which Mr. Charles Gregg left the firm, as we hoped, for ever. Then George Ruther took Horace up to a state interview with Gustav Oelrich, whose interest George thought necessary with the proprietors of the Deritend.

As they went, they stopped at the telegraph-office to leave this despatch, which they had consented to carry so far for Mr. Newland: —

BROMWICH, 10 A.M.

To First National Bank, Pittsburg:

Please take up note of Gregg & Sons for five hundred on our account. JAPHET NEWLAND.

"You can do a good deal in a forenoon," said

George to Horace, as he bade him good-by, "when every one is willing to —

"'LEND A HAND.'"

How strange it seems now to think that those two fine fellows had never spoken to each other when that day began!

CHAPTER XII.

THE DERITEND CLUB.

THIS was a good day's work already.

But George Ruther had a good deal of the Lockhard in him; and he liked to drive a bolt home, as much as the Lockhard liked to drive a dirk home.

He "made sicker" when there was a chance, on the "same afternoon."[1] And that afternoon he asked Horace to lend him the white mare in a wagon, that he might take Will Gadsden out to see Mrs. Oelrich. He had seen her husband at the counting-house in the morning. To borrow

---

[1] "The same afternoon" was a phrase I caught from the late General Mitchell, the founder of the Cincinnati Observatory. He was a most energetic person, apt to carry through what he began upon. Much of the secret of his success might be found in the frequency with which his accounts of his movements ended with this phrase, "I did "— so and so — "on the *same afternoon*."

the white mare of Horace Gregg was just a part of Ruther's thoughtfulness. It was a drop of relief to Horace to feel that he, too, could be of service to somebody.

I do not pretend but George Ruther was glad of the possible chance of seeing Bertha Oelrich as well. I do pretend that he did not go on purpose to see her.

He went to tell Mrs. Oelrich that the chances were more favorable for the "Deritend Club."

Fortune favors the brave; and the two young men found Bertha and her mother both at home. The afternoon was lovely. The golden light streamed into the conservatory, which was just now filled for the winter. There were few flowers, but there was much brilliant green. The parlor at the Oelrichs' is large and high and cheerful. The pictures are hung low, the book-cases have no glass, the easels and lolling-chairs are never twice quite in the same place; the carpet is thick, and badly faded by the perpetual sun; and, in short, you have every thing — but a "hornet's nest" — to make you comfortable. In two minutes the two young men and the two ladies were in full talk. I might say the two young ladies, for Mrs. Oelrich seems as young as her daughter.

"I thought my revolution in society was as dead as a French revolution," said she.

"Oh! they never go backwards, you know," said Mr. Ruther. "It was 'truth crushed to earth.'"

"I suppose we did not start right, mamma," said Bertha.

"My dear child, we never started at all. That was the misfortune." And Mrs. Oelrich laughed heartily.

"No," said Ruther, "you never started; but your plan was right, as ours was wrong, and I took a leaf out of your book instantly."

"Thank you, Mr. Ruther, thank you. I like to talk to such people. You and I will talk together, and let Will and Bertha talk to each other." This from Mrs. Oelrich, who then added, "Please what was the leaf, and what was the invention? Now, that they do not hear, you might confide my own secret to me."

"Why, you let the women come to your club with the men. We have now opened a regular tea-room, under John Corkery's supervision, where we serve out the strongest green tea at a cent a cup, another cent for milk and another for sugar. We encourage the lumpers and the diggers to bring round their wives to gossip in the tea-room while they smoke in the reading-room. I do not mean that all the women do it every night; but once or twice a week Betsy Flanagan or Bridget O'Toole comes round with her clean cap on, and takes what the Cheshire people call an 'outing.' There is nothing out of the way when a young fellow, walking with his sweetheart, looks in to show her a funny picture in 'Frank Leslie' or in 'Harper.' I should like to have you see the blaze of chrysanthemums and prince's-feathers and maple-leaves that John Corkery's rooms are in, which real working-women have brought in, bring in every afternoon. For those women understand very well what we are after, and they know what it is to overcome evil with good."

"Well, was that in my plan?"

"Why, of course it was. Your plan, stated in theory, is this: You substitute cheerful and animated society of both sexes for the society which exists in bar-rooms where only one sex meets; and for the society which exists in sewing-circles, where, also, only one sex meets. Now, in human life, boys and girls, and men and women, fathers and daughters, mothers and sons, like to go together, and be together."

"I thank you very heartily for making me out a philosopher," said Mrs. Oelrich. "I will make you my best courtesy when I stand up. But really I had no theory. I only remembered the 'Clarendon Club,' and thought it a shame that men should have such comforts wholly to themselves."

"Permit me," said George Ruther, laughing. "With the instinct of your sex, you saw the great void in the social life of the higher classes of American villages, and you filled it. How will that do? We could send that to the 'Journal of Intellectual Philosophy.'"

"I fall back on the sad fact that my poor club never so much as existed. We never even came to its name. That hateful 'Eagle' announced that the women were defied; and the club ceased to be."

"But you see," said Ruther, "it has come to life again. It was born in the back office of the Deritend, when Bernard Claridge 'looked forward, and not back,' and 'looked out, and not in.'"

"If you come to that," Will said,—for Will and Bertha were listening now,—"I think it was when Fanny Gregg told Bernard Claridge what the matter was!"

"Bernard Claridge and Fanny Gregg!" cried Bertha. "Why have I never seen that? So you had to get a woman to help you in all your grand plans; and a very nice and charming woman you had too."

"I never should have spoken those words," said Will. "And I am really very sorry."

"Trust me," said the bright girl. "But, Mr. Gadsden, I thought it was only women who let out secrets."

"But I am not sure that I can claim the club as mine," said Mrs. Oelrich, "if it has all these god-fathers and god-mothers."

"I wish you would talk of the club," cried Bertha. "You pretended that was what you came for; and now you talk of nothing but pretty girls and nice young men, just as if you were taking tea with Miss Hepzibah Traddles. I don't see but men are as bad as women are.

"Please talk about the club, Mr. Ruther," and she stroked the front breadths of her frock, and laid both her hands on them primly, as if she were to be lectured.

Mr. Ruther laughed this time. "We came up to make you talk about it. Perhaps Mr. Gadsden has been telling you what I have been telling your mother, that this would be a good time to begin; a good time for what Lord George Germain called 'solid operations.'

"I think," said he, "that Horace and Frank Gregg are ready for any change. They are ready to sell out, if we say so. But it would be much better to have them stay in. 'Stay-inners are of much more use in this world than come-outers,' Miss Bertha. That is a *bon-mot* of this Andrew, who was governor of Massachusetts."

"I will commit it to memory," said Bertha, "and repeat it to mamma when she wants me to take a constitutional on a rainy day."

"I think this is a good time to begin. But I think also, as Will Gadsden here has said, — I believe that we had better not begin at all, unless we can begin in force. The Greggs showed their books to Mrs. Claridge. They have shown them to me to-day. The Deritend cannot live, unless somebody, somehow, makes good the income of this bar, — that is to say, four thousand dollars a year. If we could make a club which could make that income good, why Horace and Frank Gregg are only too eager to sweep that whole bar out."

"Four thousand dollars is a good deal of money, Mr. Ruther."

"It is a great deal of money, Mrs. Oelrich. It is money very cheerfully paid, and very easily collected, when it is paid for eleven o'clocks, and comforters and smashes and treats, for cock-tails and juleps. But it would be money very hard to raise, in Bromwich or anywhere else, by a dead lift, for a mere theory of philanthropy. We ought to raise it, as the Deritend bar raises it, by giving something for something."

"We must give," said she, "something that

people like as much as they like juleps and smashes. Did you know, by the way, that they drank mint-juleps in Charles the First's time?"

"I knew the people in 'Comus' did," said he; and he quoted —

> "'And first behold this cordial julep here,
> That flames and dances in his crystal bounds,
> With spirits of balm and fragrant syrups mixed.'"

"Then you want," said Will, "to collect your money steadily, — not by jerks, — like a subscription paper."

"I cannot see," said Bertha, "how they can sell four thousand dollars' worth of this horrid whiskey."

"You would see," said Will, gravely, "if you bought it at a dollar a gallon and sold it at a dollar a quart. I think we must have two things at the club. We must have members with a regular subscription; and I hope this may not be high, for I hope the college boys will come. Then I hope that, when you and your mother want the fashionable afternoon tea, you will order it in the club parlor; when you want lunch in the village, you will order it there. And I hope that, in the winter, when you have a sociable, it will be under the club's auspices; and if you have private theatricals, they will be in the Deritend's ball-room."

"Mighty private," said Bertha.

"As private as they are in the college chapel," said Will; and Bertha owned herself vanquished.

George Ruther had been listening.

"I put all that very squarely to Horace Gregg to-day," he said. "And Gregg admits — he is very glad to admit — that the receipts of the house can be very considerably enlarged by all this sort of custom. He says it is not much, that people are unreasonable, and want to make hard bargains on such occasions. But if there were such a Deritend club as I described, and the officers really bore in mind that they were largely indebted to the house, — in short, that the house as an institution helped the club, as well as the club helped the house, — he owned that the occasional receipts of the house would be much enlarged."

"He said," cried the eager Will, "that he

would risk the chance of these things making up half what the bar pays them. Your tea and coffee, Miss Bertha, your toast, Mrs. Oelrich, my sociable tickets, and the parquet seats, we shall all buy when Mr. Ruther acts Othello. All these together will be worth two thousand dollars a year. Would you have thought that?"

"Well, mamma eats a great deal of toast, when she has been driving in the cold. For me, I never touch tea or coffee. Then we have only two thousand to see to."

"Yes," said Mr. Ruther; "but that must flow in as easily and readily as the rivers flow into the sea. There must be no hitch with begging, and fairs, and finance committees. So that we should calculate on three thousand, that we may have a margin with Mr. Newland."

"Why does that name Newland seem natural?"

"Japhet Newland was President of the Bank of England, and Marryat named a foundling after him."

"Oh! I knew I had seen it somewhere. By the way, I'll make our Mr. Newland subscribe. I won't take no for an answer. But how will you fix the subscriptions?"

THE DERITEND CLUB. 179

"I am glad you say there are to be no fairs," said Mrs. Oelrich. "I hate fairs."

"She hates them, and is all the time painting for them, and standing behind tables, and then buys half the things."

"My dear, that is one way I have of bearing my cross."

"There are worse things than fairs," said George Ruther. "They advertise a charity, and set everybody to thinking of it, and talking of it. Now a subscription paper is, or ought to be, modest, and to advertise nothing.

"But this Deritend club is not a charity. If it does not meet what Mrs. Oelrich will call a 'real void' in her Essay on American Society, we do not want it to exist at all. So we do not need a fair for it. As it starts, it must go on; acquiring its means by its own merits."

"As I mean to acquire mine, Mr. Ruther," cried Bertha.

"As I am sure you will," cried Will, with real admiration, which he was fearless about expressing.

"Two thousand dollars," said Mrs. Oelrich, pensively; "or, better, three thousand dollars every year, and no fair."

"No! but a great many people interested," said Will, hopefully.

"And a void in American society, dear mamma. Do remember the words in your own essay."

"I remember it is time for you to have on your apron, and eat your bread and milk, and kiss papa and be sent to bed."

They all laughed, and Mrs. Oelrich said again, —

"Three thousand dollars a year."

"Which is," said George Ruther, "seven hundred and fifty dollars a quarter."

"What do you say to this? added he;

"Could we not make three hundred people, say students, and school-teachers, and clerks in stores, and dress-makers, and other people that have no families, subscribe half a dollar a quarter? They would always find cheerful rooms. They would have fire, lights, newspapers, a chance to talk, and a chance to see people."

"And they would crowd your parlors so that they could not see the King of Siam, if he were there."

THE DERITEND CLUB.   181

"Why, my dear Miss Bertha, they would not all be there at one time."

"Oh, no! I forgot. They would come at different times. I beg pardon."

"Then," continued George, "could we not get a hundred subscribers who would pay more, — say two dollars a quarter, or eight dollars a year, and have the management of the thing, choose the government, appoint the committees, and so on.

"And then I should propose yet another subscription of twenty-five dollars a year, for families. This subscription would introduce strangers, and all one's family, and so on. There would not be many of these subscribers, but all there were would help. I should take such a ticket, I have so many railroad men from a distance. Your husband would take one. Dr. Witherspoon would take one. Judge Ellery would take one. We should get twenty such subscribers."

"Twenty families," said Bertha, "are five hundred dollars. A hundred annuals are eight hundred dollars. Three hundred of the college-boy kind are six hundred dollars. Six and eight are fourteen, and five are nineteen. Not enough, Mr. Ruther."

"No," he said rather abjectly, "I see it is not. And yet I had it come out quite grandly at twenty-four hundred. Perhaps I have missed something. However, we will not go off in detail. In substance, this is my idea; and I do not believe that is the hard point. I think the hard point will be to make people come to it. In as slow a town as this, it will be five years before the people most interested in this thing will know of its existence. The thing to do is to compel them to find it out."

"Without advertising it," said Bertha, "without having a fair."

Mr. Ruther was good-natured, and owned his inconsistency; and they all fell to telling what the club should have, and what it should not have.

It should have two New York papers, two or three German picture papers, the London Illustrated News (remember all this was nine years ago). It should have "Harper's Weekly" and "Monthly," and "Frank Leslie." It should have the "Atlantic," and "Godey's Ladies' Book" ("Old and New" did not then exist). It should have all the leading religious papers, — the Pittsburg and Wheeling Dailies, — our own local papers, of course.

"Do you mean to let them smoke, Mr. Ruther?" said Bertha.

"Do you mean to?" said he. "That is the real question."

"I vote for their smoking," said she, decidedly. "That is, there shall be a smoking-room, into which, of course, no woman will ever enter.

"There shall be a ladies' sanctum, into which, of course, no man shall ever enter.

"There shall be a parlor, as pretty as mamma knows how to make it, into which ladies and gentlemen shall both enter.

"There shall be a library, as cosey and convenient as you men know how to make, into which gentlemen and ladies both shall enter. Then there shall be a coffee-room, where mamma will eat her toast, and I will sometimes order a grilled humming-bird's wing by way of encouraging the club."

Her father had come in while she was talking. When she stopped, he went on : —

"I think there had better be a blue satin arm-chair, with gold legs, on a slight dais, and a canopy over it, of blue silk with tassels, for Miss Bertha Oelrich to sit upon."

"And another by its side, of dark crimson satin, with the legs a little longer, for Mr. Gustav Oelrich to sit on, and keep his daughter in order." As Bertha said this, she jumped from her chair, kissed her father, made him sit in her place, and took her own upon his knee.

"Tell me all about this treason," said he.

And in much less time, and what the vernacular calls much shorter metre, than I could tell it in, Bertha told him.

Mr. Oelrich was interested through and through. But, from the first moment, he took a much broader and more fearless view of their plans than they had done.

"You see," said he, "you are going to work without capital. That is a mistake young women make, my dear," and he kissed her. "Now you must provide certain things, which are to remain, by your capital stock. As soon as you have any capital, the people who have subscribed it will want to get their money's worth, and they will follow the thing up, and believe in it, and come to meetings so as to show to themselves, and to other people too, that they have not thrown their money away. I shall do so. If you made me give you twenty-five dollars for my annual subscription, I should only laugh at you, and should never go into the club room. But when I have subscribed two or three hundred dollars, and have made Hans Otterbein do the same, and Judge Ellery and Mr. Newland, I shall be so afraid they will be dissatisfied that I shall be smoking bad cigars and reading the 'Saturday Review' at the club all the time."

George Ruther was greatly interested. "Do not suppose that I did . not think of this?" said he.

"Yes, Mr. Ruther, you thought of it, but you did not dare. You saw what a drowsy place Bromwich is, and perhaps you thought it was as poor as it pretends to be. The truth is that there are twenty people here who have yet to learn the luxury of public spirit, — of doing something for other people while they do it for themselves. And this club of my little Bertha's will be an excellent place for them to break the ice."

"Mamma will be very jealous, if you call it my club," said Bertha. "It is all her invention."

"I'll risk your mamma, my dear. I should like to inquire of you, who are, I believe, chief of staff at the Oelrich club, at what time tea is expected in that establishment."

But at that moment the tea-bell rang, and Mrs. Oelrich led the way to that entertainment which surpasses any banquet of Lucullus, the "high tea" of a good housekeeper on her mettle.

CHAPTER XIII.

THE SOCIAL REVOLUTION.

"HAD Mr. Ruther sent the mare home before you went to bed, Frank?" This was Horace's question to his brother the next morning.

Frank laughed, and said that at quarter past eleven the mare and the wagon had not been heard from.

So much evidence was there that the young gentlemen in their visit at Mr. Oelrich's had had a "good time."

For, indeed, at tea-time, and once and again after tea, the talk had run back to the Deritend club; and, as one and another evening visitor came in, Mr. Gustav Oelrich had new opportunity for seeing how his larger plans would strike them. He talked more and more definitely, as he went on. And, indeed, his knowledge of men, of affairs, and of Bromwich men and Bromwich affairs in particular, made his advice of much more worth than that of the younger men could be. By the time Mr. Ruther and Will proposed to retire, he was in full blast with paper before him, — schedules of purchases, drafts of a constitution, — and he called them back to discuss this detail, and that, and another, till it was, indeed, eleven o'clock before they said their last good-bys.

"I do not know when I have seen two finer fellows," said he, as with the ladies he turned back from the door, after the young men had driven away. "I always liked what little I saw of Will Gadsden, and mighty sorry I was for him when he broke down. But this friend of his, or of yours, Bertha, is a great acquisition to the town. Prescott told me he thought they had a treasure in him; but I do not think Prescott understood how much of a man he is, how accomplished a gentleman he is."

"I do not think Mr. Prescott could understand, papa."

"Oh, you must not be hard upon Prescott, puss. Wait till he has shared his last crust with you, as he has with me, and you will not grudge him the privilege of an occasional blunder in his grammar."

" As many as you like, papa, if he only talks to you, and not to me. Good-night, good-night. I really feel as if the evening had done something."

And the next day, and the next, showed that it had done something. Mr. Oelrich had taken up the Deritend club with a will. He was well pleased with his own scheme of a capital large enough to buy all the furniture and fixtures, and to yield a little income against a rainy day. At the first meeting of the bank directors, he talked the scheme "into" them. Then he made it in his way to see the three or four magnates who owned the Deritend House, and he talked his schemes into them. He was one of the people who are used to having things succeed. He never permitted them to fail, indeed; and this the little world of Bromwich knew very well. And, when he intimated his confidence in the success of his own plans by subscribing five hundred dollars to a capital stock of five thousand, it was clear enough to Japhet Newland, to Dr. Witherspoon, to Judge Ellery, and to my uncle Dr. Claridge, that he was fully in earnest, knew this thing could succeed, and meant that it should.

Ruther and one or two of his companions, to whom a hundred dollars was of more account than ten thousand were to these magnates, avouched their faith by taking each a share of the capital at a hundred dollars. Three or four widowed ladies — one, alas! who had reason, in a desolate home, to wish there had never been any bar-room in Bromwich — took each a single share. The Baptist Sewing Society, the Methodist Charity Committee, and the Presbyterian Sewing Circle, all composed of women, made each their respective ministers shareholders. And thus, in two or three weeks, the existence of the club was made sure by five subscriptions to its stock of five hundred dollars; one of three hundred, six of two hundred, and ten of one hundred each. There were fifty shares in all.

Judge Ellery, Mr. Oelrich, and George Ruther were trustees who held this money, and were to appoint their own successors.

Thus fortified, the trustees went boldly forward, and hired the whole of the ground floor of the north wing of the Deritend House for an annual rent of two thousand dollars, which carried with it the condition that while they occupied these premises no liquor should be sold at any bar in the house, nor should any liquor be sold to be carried from the house. It was admitted that a *bona fide* traveller might order liquor in his rooms or at his meals, and that while the house held a taverner's license it might fill this order. But this permission was not to cover the service of liquor for parties of guests, and the keepers of the house bound themselves to restrict this sale to persons who were really transient travellers, who bought for their own use.

The rent would have been enormous, had it not brought with it this condition. With the condition, all parties considered it fair.

The north wing was, on the whole, not badly arranged for the club's purposes. It contained the old bar-room, the billiard-room, the reading-room, and two or three rather inconvenient private parlors. But, by knocking away one or two partitions, they would be able to have substantially Bertha Oelrich's *sine qua non;* namely, a sanctum for the women at one end, a sanctum for the men at the other, a coffee-room, a drawing-room, and a library beside the billiard-room.

Having gone thus far, and the gossip of the town being now at the very keenest on the matter, the shareholders drew up their constitution, and offered it for signature. I copy it from a musty old paper, which has not seen the light for years.

The Deritend Club

Is established to promote better society among the gentlemen and ladies of Bromwich. It will occupy for the present the rooms rented for the purpose in the Deritend House.

No person shall join the club till his or her name has been presented for at least one week by some member. If one-fourth of the members vote against the candidate in that time, the candidate is not elected, and cannot be named again for one year.

The officers, till otherwise ordered, are a president, treasurer, secretary, and three directors. The six constitute the board of management, and are chosen semi-annually.

Voting members of the club will pay an annual assessment of eight dollars.

Members who do not wish to vote will pay an

annual assessment of two dollars, payable quarterly. Heads of families may take family tickets to the clubrooms for twenty-five dollars, if elected members. But such membership carries but one vote.

BROMWICH, Nov. 11, 1865.

With this programme, the twenty-two shareholders met and voted for members. They chose in eventually the greater part of the town. They chose all the college-boys, all the clerks in all the stores, and all their masters. Ruther brought up lists of the railroad men, and they chose all of them. They chose every girl in every paper-box factory and in every mantua-maker's shop. Unless, on a week's inquiry, something turned up to the disadvantage of a person named, they chose in him or her. They had a list of nearly a thousand people, who had wit enough to be on the voting list, or to subscribe for some newspaper, or to belong to some sewing circle. The shareholders had no desire to keep people out, but to bring them in.

At the first election they chose about three hundred people, trying to keep the numbers of men and women equal. They sent to each of them a circular explaining the plan of the club, which they all knew very well before, and asked them to meet, only two days after, in the club parlors. Well, a great many did meet. The college-boys came in great force. Enough voting members joined to choose a set of officers, and to ballot for more members. Once a week they met to vote for more. And then things went briskly on.

Dr. Claridge was chosen President.

Gustav Oelrich was Treasurer.

Bertha Oelrich was Secretary.

George Ruther, William Gadsden, and Fanny Gregg were Directors.

Then these people appointed Committees on Membership, Committee on Library, Committee on Coffee-Room, Committee on Ladies' Room, Committee on Smoking-Room, with Committees on Furniture, on Newspapers, and, — oh I do not know what there were not committees on! And with such an Executive, and the thorough interest of the town, you may be sure that these committees were by no means slow in their duties.

Well, if you want to see what the club rooms

proved to be, you had better come to Bromwich and see them; though, to be sure, they are twice as large now as they were then.

The billiard-room they left much as they found it, only they put a new paper on the walls and cocoa matting on the floor.

The women, under Mrs. Oelrich, did their best on the drawing-room; and the men, led by Will and by Bernard, did their best on the library. And, for Bromwich, very pretty rooms they were and are. No lack of coal in Bromwich, and cheerful fires blazed in those gigantic grates all winter long.

What mysteries were in the ladies' sanctum, nay, what comforts were in the men's smoking-room, it is not for these pages to describe. Let Jenkins tell.

What I have to describe is

THE SOCIAL REVOLUTION.

With every paper-hanger who worked on parlor or library, with every bale of carpet which came from Cincinnati, when the grand piano arrived from Steinway, and when the boxes of books from

Appleton's began to arrive, the public interest and excitement waxed keener and keener. When a tall cheval glass from Philadelphia was unpacked, — such as was not known in Bromwich before, — there was new amazement; and each of the novelties, whether great or small, was an advertisement of the club. At last the upholstering and furnishing were over, the newspapers and magazines directed to "The Deritend Club" began to arrive. The men who in America are called fresco-painters, because they do not paint in fresco, took down their tall frameworks, and showed the beautiful ceilings they had worked upon. With new brooms the tidy chambermaids of the Deritend swept the new carpets. Fresh flowers from the Oelrich conservatories, and from the Ellerys' and the Rittenhouses', and even from the far-away Watsons', blazed on the tables and mantels. The latest "London Spectator," "Punch," and "Saturday Review" were on the green tables, with a "Grenzboten" for Hans Otterbein, and a "Revue des Deux Mondes" for Dr. Witherspoon.

Long before this time the first hundred members had chosen many hundred more members from that catholic list I told you of. To each person chosen a printed invitation had been sent; and a great many of them had joined the club at once. Still, more than half of them had made no sign.

It was not therefore till this night, when, as I say, the pretty parlor and the cosey reading-room blazed with flowers and glowed with hospitable fires, that we knew whether the "Social Revolution" would go forward.

Mrs. Oelrich always hoped, but while she hoped she sometimes feared. But four persons never feared for an instant. They were Will Gadsden, pretty Fanny Gregg, and her two brothers. "Fanny," said Horace, "this house will be swamped with people. They have no idea how many of their invitations will be accepted. I know the pulse of this town better than they do." And Fanny and Clara bestirred themselves. While dear Mrs. Gregg presided over the forces in the club rooms, and dusted here and directed there, and consulted Bertha, and agreed with Bertha's mother, those nice girls and their brothers, with an attached throng of the servants, were privately decorating every room in each wing of the ground floor of the house, and were making all their part of it cheerful and glad. It would be hard to say where Clara got her flowers. Not from the grand conservatories, but from Miss Etter's frames and Mary Freeland's windows and Aunt Rachel's parlors. And Bernard and half the Sophomores had privily collected prince's-pine for her, and every press in Bromwich had given up its treasures of colored maple and sumac for her. Every room was festooned with wreaths and green pennons of her prince's-pine, and the spaces within glowed with her crimson and gold. Over the carpet of the ladies' large drawing-room she had a faultless white linen dancing carpet. All these preparations Fanny and Clara had carried on without fuss, and, indeed, without the knowledge of the hard-working parties in the club room.

The Deritend Club Rooms were to be opened to the Club on Christmas eve. So read the cards. And as early as five Hans Otterbein and Mrs. Otterbein and all the little Otterbeins were unloaded from the great double sleigh in which they had been driven in. The tidy "page in waiting," as the black boy chose to call himself, from some novel he had picked up in a "New York Weekly," showed them to the cloak-rooms, and, to Hans Otterbein's amazement, gave him tickets for his coat and hat and fur gloves. The president and all the officers and the committee of reception were on duty to receive. Gustav Oelrich delighted Mrs. Otterbein by talking German to her, and, in the most matter-of-fact way, set to work to explain to her what comforts and conveniences she was to receive from the club rooms every time she came to town to do her shopping. How she would not have to wait at that stupid Dietrich's shop till he had made up her parcel; how it would be quite enough if she just left her order at Walworth's; how she could run on, if she wanted, to the High School, and see if the children were going forward to her mind; and then she could come round to the club and warm her feet and heat her soapstone, and be all ready for the boys to join her when school was over, — and here would be the parcel from Walworth, and the parcel from Dietrich, and no danger that she would leave either of them anywhere.

Like most people in this world, Mrs. Otterbein understood the concrete instance much better than any abstract theory.

"Ah, you have heard my poor story?" said she.

No: Mr. Oelrich had not heard it at all. And then there followed a long story, how she had left a parcel at Tunstall the butcher's, but she supposed she had left it at Clark and Vanderwall's, and so on and so on. And she began to see, what she had never seen before, that the Deritend Club was to come into her staid and matronly life, and was not a mere device for boys and girls who wanted dancing, or people, like her husband, who wanted to read the newspapers.

Meanwhile, the "page in waiting," and many other pages in waiting, all wearing the pretty button-hole bouquets which Bertha had provided, were at their wits' end to hurry people up fast enough, and to dismiss in order the sleighs which followed fast upon each other at the doors. Whatever the village people meant to do about the Deritend Club, it was clear enough that the people at Faff's and at the Gap and on the Lower Level, nay, that even all the Watsonville people, meant to patronize it. They had found out the use of a place to warm their fingers in on a cold day. Frank Gregg, as I have said, was not caught surprised nor unprepared. He had a full force in his own stables, and he was ready with the stalls at Urquhart's livery, and at Brown's also. And, though Frank would ask no favors of Readhead at the "Northern," his stable-boys were on perfectly good terms with their stable-boys, and that lazy Readhead never knew how many horses came through his stable-yard that night and were sheltered in his great empty barn. But so many of the country people came, and they came so early, and they seemed so well pleased, — they sat down so resolutely to look at the plates in the Cyclopædias and the prints in "Punch" and "Harper's Weekly" and the "Illustrated News," taking in very completely that these things were theirs, and were what they had paid their money for, — so many of them were there, I say, and so comfortable were they, that

Bertha at seven o'clock came to George Ruther in utter despair.

"Dear Mr. Ruther, what shall we do? These rooms are as full as they will hold; and there is not one person from the village here yet. I have told everybody I saw not to come a minute before seven; and now all our accommodations are taken up, and, when they come, they will not see one of their pretty things."

"The more, the merrier," said he; but he looked puzzled and rueful as she did, and they both laughed.

"Better too many than too few, mamma says," said Bertha, more pensively. "And it is not three hours since she was sure that there would not be fifty people here. Don't you think it would do to tell some of these good folks that they must give room to others? That woman has sat in that easy-chair an hour, if she has sat a minute there."

"But she may sit there a month, under the by-laws of the club," said Ruther, as ruefully as before.

"And yet they keep pouring in!" said poor

Bertha. "I threw open the coffee-room before they were ready there, but that was only a moment's respite. As for the billiard-room, I believe they will have to stand on the tables, or sit under them. Really, Mr. Ruther, we should have fitted the rooms with galleries," and she wrung her hands in mock agony.

"Gadsden," said Ruther, beckoning to Will to come nearer, "what is to happen to us? We shall be trampled under the feet of enraged clubbists. We shall be fighting for the right to approach the window, as they did at the Black Hole of Calcutta. They come, and come, and come! Don't you wish you had blackballed all the last nomination?"

"Not I," said Will, triumphantly. "Let them come as the leaves of Vallombrosa come! But, if this is club-life, they must be queer people, if they like it. And do you know, George, this is hardly the beginning? There are not ten college-boys here!"

"It is all that we are so hopelessly agreeable," said Bertha. "'This fatal gift of beauty,' as Mrs. Radcliffe says. Can't you disguise your charms a little, Mr. Gadsden? Can't you look fierce for once, and drive them away?"

"There!" cried Ruther: "somebody has made a diversion." And the crowd swayed into the drawing-room at the sound of some bold loud chords on the great piano.

It was Susie Claridge who had undertaken this entertainment of the guests, and who had chosen the Grand March in Faust to dedicate the new piano by. Close to the instrument the throng in that room pressed to listen; and Bertha and George Ruther both — so soon as they knew who was playing, as they did, of course, in a moment — looked stealthily on Will Gadsden's face, and then caught each other's eyes as they looked away from it. Poor fellow! he had not heard Susie play, now, for so long! It was not strange that his eyes flashed so!

The library or reading-room was a little cleared for a moment by the throng which thus pressed into the drawing-room. But neither Bertha nor Will had exaggerated. The cry was still "They come," and no one went away. Not one Watsonville visitor dreamed of going. "If there were any thing more to eat," said Bertha, "I could understand their staying for it. But surely they have had all the tea they wanted; and poor Miss Ellery must be dead at her tea-table before this. I have not dared go in there for an hour!"

Susie tried one and another bright, hearty march or waltz; and then Frank Brannan took her place at the piano, and he and Hooper began to sing. They have rich voices, and they sung a little ballad of Hooper's, —

"Let me tell you, boys, the story,
Of the dark and bloody land," —

and they sang it well. The room was fairly hushed to listen; and, when they came to the end, more than one of the old farmers was crying.

In the library there was more breathing room. Horace Gregg found Ruther and Gadsden and Bertha, and said: "I don't want to interrupt; but I am so glad to find any one in authority. You will be crowded to death here: you have not half your people yet. I foresaw all this; and have some music in the great ladies' parlor. Shall I tell them to play?"

"Horace Gregg, you are a trump," said Ruther, in admiration.

"Mr. Gregg," said Bertha, "you shall be crowned by every girl on the committee. You have saved the life of I don't know how many citizens. I was dying of mortification at our miscalculations."

"Ah, Miss Oelrich, there are never too many guests, when they are only friends." And he held up his hand, stood on tiptoe so as to catch the eye of Sam, his faithful squire, — who waited on the stairway, watching him, — and he, the moment he saw the signal, flung open the doors of the great ladies' drawing-room of the hotel, — not one of the club rooms, — and at the instant the band which Frank Gregg had secreted there began to play.

No! they did not play the overture to Fidelio. They played "Hail Columbia," and they played it very well. It was the Shelbyville band, who had been smuggled into town by Frank and Horace Gregg, resolved to have their part in the entertainment. And so busy were we club managers in our arrangements that we had not seen nor guessed that the House was making its arrangements on a much broader and more business-like scale than we.

Bertha clapped her hands with delight. "And yet I don't know why I am surprised, Mr. Gregg: for this is just like you, if half what your friends say is true of you." And she held out her hand to him. This was their introduction to each other. Then she blushed, and he blushed. But he rallied, and offered her his arm, and walked with her into the great ladies' parlor, — as I must call it, to distinguish it from the club parlor, — and there presented her to his mother and father; and there she found Fanny and Clara, his sisters, and praised them with all her heart, as women can, when they will, for the beauty and the surprise of their decorations.

"To think, you witches, that, while your mother was slaving herself to death with us, you were so quietly making a garden out of these rooms, and keeping your work secret to the last. Yet you appeared, Fanny, from time to time, as a manager should; and I had no thought that any such marvels were going on."

Fanny confessed that they had many hands to help them, and that she did not know where they should have been but for the Sophomores.

The crash of music from the band soon drew the crowd out into the spacious halls, and into the great hotel drawing-rooms. Dr. Claridge himself came up with a pretty Mrs. Templeman from Washington, the wife of the Senator, to whom he was making the agreeable, and showing the lions as to the most distinguished stranger in town. The Doctor had not had much to do with our upholstering and furnishing, but he knew enough of it to know what he was to call attention to. The diversion into the larger rooms brought as much satisfaction to him as to the rest of the managers. And to lead that diversion, so far as he might, he led the way with his guest.

So they entered among the first from their side, and came full upon pretty Fanny Gregg with her attendants. She was looking prettier than ever, as her face flushed a little with the success of her surprise, and their eager thanks for the relief; and she looked her very best, as the president of the club made his acknowledgments to her.

"Dear Dr. Claridge," said she, very prettily, "you forget that I am a director in the Deritend Club also, though one of the humblest of directors. What duty have I to-night but to help forward the inauguration?"

"I must certainly compliment you, my dear Doctor, on your choice of directors," said Mrs. Templeman. "We shall all be converted to Women's Rights, if you always give us such nice public servants as Miss Gregg and Mrs. Oelrich."

The Doctor told her that he quite agreed with her in her estimate of his subordinates, and said that for a very little club, say to take a sleigh-ride together, or eat a leg of mutton together, he would not ask for a better selection than his five officers and directors. This gave him an opportunity to present George Ruther to Mrs. Templeman, and Ruther then took her off to show her some of Miss Gregg's remarkable tupelos, hackmatacks, and hornbeams. So Dr. Claridge, on his part, had a chance to offer Fanny Gregg his arm, and to walk round her rooms with her, talking to her first about what the Sophomores had done, and then, as I guessed, on matters much more central and vital. To the immense interest of half Bromwich, the president of the club was before long seated on a sofa in the corner of the room, talking to the daughter of the hotel-keeper as eagerly as ever he talked to a student who had come up for advice to his sanctum, and talking at the same time in tones so low that, even had any one been rude in that assembly, no one could have guessed what the subject was. And Fanny Gregg was evidently as eager, and after a minute as unconscious, as was he.

Meanwhile to George Ruther, as they walked, Mrs. Templeman said: "It's all nonsense, Mr. Ruther. I spent five years in Europe. I have lived in Paris, I have lived in Vienna. I was three months in Edinboro.' I was six months in Berlin. I have spent the season in London. I have spent a season in Geneva, and I was a winter in Rome. Well, you will know what I mean, so I am not afraid to say that I had great advantages there. My father was a minister of our government, and we had all the advantages the diplomatic service gives. I had young friends enough, friends of very early days, to

THE SOCIAL REVOLUTION. 211

be well received everywhere. And I was well received. I know I was. I have enjoyed life very much wherever I have been, never more than I enjoy it now at Washington.

"Still, Mr. Ruther, if you talk of Society, and mean 'Society,' the best society I have ever seen was in a manufacturing town of ten thousand people."

"Where? in England or Scotland?"

"Oh, dear, no!" said she: "I do not know what they have there. This was in America, not a thousand miles from where we are to-day."

"I think I know what you mean."

"I mean this: that if there were a bright young lawyer, we all knew him; if there were a Norwegian in a wire-mill, who could read Bishop Tegner, we knew that; if there were a clever girl in a public school, who drew well or sang well, we knew her; if there were a nice Quaker girl, who had that divine gift for acting that some Quaker girls have, we knew her; if there were a young Baptist minister, who was in correspondence with the patriarch of Russia, we knew him; and if there were a young doctor, who knew where to find Mayflowers half an hour before the rest of us, we knew him. Don't you see, when a place is as small as that place was, there is some chance for society? But society is impossible in London or Vienna, unless you take it in coteries, and coteries cannot be many-sided."

"The town must be small; but it must be bright, Mrs. Templeman."

"I have found no Americans who were not bright enough," said she. "The trouble with us is, that having no native gift for society, and having great gifts for other things, say for subduing the world, we get so tired with them that we let the society go. There is my husband. Tired to death with acting as the petty attorney for all his constituents, he tells me to take the carriage and to leave his cards for him, and then he says that the society of Washington is dull. The truth is that the real society of Washington is almost incomparably good, for reasons you understand. But he knows no more about it, after seven years, than I know of the society of Pekin."

"Yet Washington is better than any other large American city," said Ruther.

"Was before the war, may be again," said she. "For there is no other place known to me, where the men do not want to work after four o'clock in the afternoon. Therein Washington has one great advantage. Have you put on an eight-hour law in Bromwich?"

"No," said he, laughing; "but, if you will not publish it in the newspaper, I have great hopes that this club may do so. If Mr. Oelrich there, or Professor Webber there, or Judge Ellery there, or much more Converse and Wayland, and those ambitious young lawyers, can spend an hour a day here and not lose reputation, there is an hour a day saved for each of them, and three or four years added to each of their lives. And if, as time passes, women as mature and agreeable as Mrs. Claridge, and Mrs. Ellery, and Mrs. Halliday, and Mrs. Templeman, will think it is not beneath them to spend an hour here occasionally, why such men as these will give the hour to the club. Its real success depends, as the success of every thing else depends, on the women, and on the best women of the town."

"I am sure the women are much obliged to you

in general," said she, "and Mrs. Templeman in particular. But we will not stop to compliment. Do you know that Mr. Sarmiento said to me " —

And they swept on.

Meanwhile Mr. Oelrich and Bertha and Frank Gregg had organized a dozen or more quadrilles in the great ladies' drawing-room; the dancing enthusiasm had spread to the adjacent public drawing-room; the band had sent its fiddlers to the front, and spirited dancing-music was beginning. All this drew even a larger number of the young people away from the club rooms proper, and the company left in them was just large enough to make them cheerful and sociable, and to show just what they were and what they were meant for. In the great ladies' drawing-room, Dr. Claridge was still in his everlasting and unconscious *tête-à-tête* with Fanny Gregg on the sofa in the corner. On the other sofas were a few matrons sitting well pleased; but, excepting the dancers, hardly another person in the room. Bernard was here and there and everywhere, taking directions from the leader of the band, pushing head couples here and foot couples there, when a shy Sophomore, with a shyer little country girl for a partner, beckoned him and said that they had no *vis-à-vis*, and asked him to find one.

"Surely," said Bernard; and he rushed on to the hall to pounce on the first man he might, before he waved his hand to the band.

The first man of course was Will Gadsden. "Will, Will! find some girl and come and dance here, just to start them."

"Oh, any thing but that, Bern!" said poor Will, and his face fell for the first time that evening.

Bernard cursed himself for saying just the wrong thing, as usual. But he did not forget what he was after. Still it seemed as if there were nobody in the hall but German stock-raisers and veterans of the Thirty Years' War, certainly nobody whom Bernard dared ask to dance. He plunged back into the drawing-room, and found his sister Susie listening to Mrs. Otterbein's account of the epidemic among her chickens.

"Susie," said Bernard, "do let me bring you somebody to dance with, so as to make up this set."

"Oh, any thing but that, Bern!" said poor Susie, and her face fell for the first time that evening. And again Bernard cursed himself for a fool.

He told the Sophomore he must take the side of the quadrille, and must find his own *vis-à-vis*, while the head and foot went through the figure. Then he waved his hand to his leader of the music, whatever son of Korah that might be, ran to Clara Gregg, who was his own partner, looked round once more, half-puzzled, as he wondered what his father and Fanny could be talking about and crying about, and so the dancing began.

And now the first germs of club life showed themselves, — oh, how timidly! But then and there "Society" was born in Bromwich, and the "Social Revolution" began. The billiard-room was then much too large for the four tables in it; and the committee had put at the two ends eight inlaid chess-tables, and furnished them with regulation chess-men, ordered by Will from the Place Palais Royal. Here was a nice nut-brown girl, who had bravely brought an "Illustrated News" in her hand, and had set out a problem for herself, to try to solve it. She had, of her own free spirit, achieved that greatest of discoveries, that nobody was looking at her, thinking of her, or caring one penny whether she lived or died. To the next table came a frightened Senior, who had joined the club that he might read French newspapers, and now was so terrified in the reading-room, lest any one should see him reading a French newspaper, and might think he was "squirting," that he had retired into the furthest corner of the billiard-room, and was inventing a problem for himself there. As he went on with his problem, he saw the nut-brown girl bring in hers. He turned his back to her, and went on. When, of a sudden, scales fell from his eyes also! Was it some burst of laughter from the coffee-room? Was it some memory of something he had read in the Greek Reader, that the bashful man is a proud fool? Was it "gospel light in Bullen's eyes"? Do not ask me. I do not know. But he also was converted to the great law of the universe. With courage surpassing that which crossed the bridge of Lodi, he turned and walked to the other table, and said, "When you have finished your problem, will you play with me, Miss Marston, though I play very badly?" The last word choked in his throat, like the last death-gasp of an athlete in the arena. Still Mary Marston understood, swept her problem off the board, and for two hours they two did the thing they liked best in the whole world.

In the coffee-room Miss Ellery was in her element. She was joking, laughing, scolding, ordering, sympathizing, snubbing, repenting, and apologizing. Dry old gentlemen, like Japhet Newland, and even Aaron Roscommon himself, who had not been to a party for years, sat around her with dry old ladies, the partners of their youth when men danced "Hull's Victory" and the "Lancashire Lass." And though the caps of these ladies were stiff, and though it was difficult to account whether for the contrasts or the harmonies in their ribbons, every one of them felt as young, my dear Lily, and my dear Ben, and my dear Helen, as you do on this living Christmas morning when you read of them. And so did the Judge and Japhet Newland and the other old-time admirers.

At the piano, in the ladies' room, there sat Hannah Guilders, a bright girl from the cloakroom at Clark and Vanderwall's, delighted to play on an instrument which was really finer than any other in town. And around her were a group of young people, with "Do try this," and "Do try that, Hannah," turning over one and another book of glees or of hymn-tunes, or one and another sheet of music, which had been provided as the beginning of the club's musical library. Here was old Judge Ellery himself, beaming as he listened.

"How little it takes to make young folks happy, Mr. Newland."

And in one corner were two or three girls puzzling over a "Bazar." This was before the days of "Harper's Bazar," I think. I am sure, at least, that this was a German copy. Here were the mysterious dots, and the manifold secrets, all imprinted on the same page; here were the puzzles, the problems, and all the rest, but all the text was German; and these girls, who could not read a word of German, were trying to make out how this and that could be, from mere force of will and ingenuity. When, as I live, there is Hosea Withers, the most solemn of Divinity students, who spent all last year in Halle, deep in Dogmatik, not quite telling them what is the German for "girl" and what is the German for "pretty," but still actually explaining how it must be meant that this gore shall fit into that angle, and translating for them all the intricate instructions about three needles and four loops, casting off two stitches and knitting three!

If Hosea Withers can do that, we need not despair for the reconstruction of society! We shall see Professor Middleage himself teaching Miss Julia Clark how to frost her hearts and how to "dorer" her rounds!

So for eager, cheerful, surprising hours upon hours, the evening of the dedication of the rooms sped by.

At nine o'clock there came a second surprise. All through the evening the coffee-room had been in full blast, with such refreshments as the club expected to be prepared to furnish from hour to hour of its working life, as was fully explained in programme B, which had been distributed among the members. "Neither more nor less than every-day work," — Mr. Oelrich said, — "we put our best foot foremost, but our worst foot is as good as our best." And people had paid for what they ate and drank, or had opened their account on the club books, all according to the ordinances for such cases made and provided. This was all the "entertainment," as a carnal world calls "victuals and drink," which the managers had planned. But at nine o'clock Mr. Charles Gregg, with all his own suavity of deportment, had come to Dr. Claridge, and had asked him if he would be so good as to lead Mrs. Oelrich out to supper; had intimated that if the Doctor would leave Fanny, to whom he had again frozen, somebody else would take care of her. At the same moment the band struck up a march, the great doors of the great hotel dining-room were thrown open, and there, to be sure, was supper served for the whole company; and, in procession, the whole company followed the president and the vice-president to the feast. This was the second surprise achieved by the hosts of the house, in their care for the guests of the club and the club itself. The secret had been well kept, and the surprise was complete and brilliant.

The fame of it cleared the club library and the drawing-room. And when Will Gadsden, only afraid that some timid dressmaker or more timid academy boy might have lingered in the one room or the other, passed rapidly through billiard-room, library, and drawing-room, he saw only Bertha, as she entered the last of these rooms on the same errand with himself.

He gave her both hands; and they stood and looked each other in the face, laughing.

"You came to hunt for stragglers," said he; "but there are no stragglers here. I have hunted both those rooms through, and looked into the coffee-room."

"The crash of the march called them all," said she: "was it not good in Horace Gregg? And how they must have worked, all of them, really with their own hands, all day!"

"I saw Horace, just now, at the office. And I think he is the handsomest, happiest fellow I ever saw. Oh, dear! I could not but go back to that wretched morning, which — which I could not speak of but that you know it all." And he led her across the room to the fire; and she sat, not unwilling, in one of the deep lolling-chairs, and let him move a smaller chair for himself to her side.

"Is it not good to sit down for just a minute, and to be sure they are all taken care of?" cried she. "Mr. Gadsden, was there ever any thing so successful?"

"It could not be better," said he. "I suppose you imagined it, but I did not. The half was not told me, nor the quarter of a half. What I did not expect was that everybody would fit in so exactly. You see — well, all is that I was a fool. Somehow, I supposed that, because I had been in England, and had dined at the Union League in New York, I knew how to act at our little club, and that I could teach them. And just so, — of course, I was a fool: they knew what they were about a hundred times better than I did."

"That's it precisely," said Bertha. "When I saw one of those Divinity students explaining to Jane Furness how she was to knit a chair-tidy, then I said, 'Nunc dimittis.' I then and there resolved that I would never think the work of the world rested on me again. Oh, dear me! Will, do you remember that day when I took you into the carriage. How little while it was ago."

And by this time Miss Bertha Oelrich's face was fire. For although all these girls used to call him "Will," when he entered college with Bernard Claridge, and they were themselves in the academy, and although "Bertha" and "Will" had lasted till his disgrace, she had not, of course, broken any barrier in this fashion, not in all the conferences and intimacies of the Directorate, of the room-furnishing, and of endless walks, rides, and committee-meetings.

Will did his best, and with a certain success, not to seem to notice the slip, and to go on as if nothing had happened. But he did notice it, and he "worked on nerve" for a good many words, before he spoke easily again.

"How little while to be sure!" said he; "and yet it seems, in some things it seems, as if we were in another world! Poor Mrs. Meiers,—think of the change there! John Corkery,—think of all that! Ruther, too,"—and his face beamed with the Uriel rapture,—" to think that I scarcely knew that man that day! How did I ever live without the — well, I can't talk about Ruther, Miss Bertha. But, when I come home to work after a walk with him, every thing seems so clear, and I am another man."

It was Will Gadsden who had forgotten himself now, and it was Miss Bertha who was trying to look properly indifferent, as she listened to praises of Mr. George Ruther, which she would not have trusted herself to utter, nor even own to herself that she took pleasure in. But she had to say something too. How steadfastly our good breeding holds us to our work! and she succeeded in saying, —

"Come to work, Mr. Gadsden! You do not pretend that you have done any work in the last two months, excepting direct those paper-hangers and scold the carpet-men?"

"Why, of course, it does not amount to much; but, then, what am I here for, Miss Oelrich? I must go to my lectures, you know; and Judge Ellery and Professor Howland and Mr. Carleton do expect something."

"And you have really been studying since this club was formed?"

"Not as hard as I wish I had, but I have not been behindhand."

"Studying!" cried the impetuous girl. "Studying law, in that den of yours upstairs, just as if there were no club, no application for license, no Phi Nu, no notes going to protest, no Horace Gregg!" She longed to say, "No Susie Claridge." But this time she held herself in check.

"No! not that," said he: "I won't brag, Miss Bertha; but I will say that I have studied twenty times harder and to more purpose than I could have done, or should have done, but for these things, — the terrible things or the good things. Here you know," now he spoke more confidentially, and he had indeed forgotten himself in her sympathy, — "here, you know, every thing is real, and close at hand. Now, at Heidelberg, the whole motive of my life was three thousand miles away. Here it is my own language and my own home."

His eyes were filling with tears, and, for that matter, hers were too.

"Oh, Miss Bertha, there is not a step that I take in this house but reminds me of what I threw away here. I cannot do the least kindness to one of those shy students, but the boy is I myself; and it is Dr. Claridge or Mrs. Claridge, or she herself, who is saying some kind, encouraging word to me. And then, you see of course, it is madness to think how I threw all such kindness away; and it would be death itself, but that God makes us hope and tells us to forget. And, of course, I swear a hundred times a day that, if I can make a career, or can redeem a character, I will; that I will do it here, and that one day she shall not be ashamed that I loved her, and love her, as no man ever loved woman before!

"But, Miss Oelrich, I never ought to have said this to you. Only it is a blessing to say it to somebody."

Bertha was pale with excitement, and her eyes overflowing with tears. But she held her hand out and gave it to him, and said: "Will, I thank you with all my heart for saying it, and I thank God for teaching you to say it. Only I wish it had been said to one other person before you said it to me. But, Will," she said again, "you are sure of one friend, who will pray for you every night, and hope for you every day; and that is I.

I call you 'Will' on purpose now," she added proudly.

"And you will promise me"—

"I will promise you any thing, every thing. I have implicit confidence in you, Will."

"Thank you," said he, and he bent over and kissed her hand, as if this were a covenant. "Then promise me that you will never by word or token let her know, or any one know, that I have said to you what I have said."

"Oh, Will, that is hard."

"Hard, but it must be, you see! If ever that saint comes to know that I am new-born and another man, she must find it for herself, and not because I have said so. Talk is so easy!" He said this with all Abdiel's scorn.

"I have promised," said Bertha, "and what I promise I perform. But I am sure you are all wrong. You ought to let me, at least, tell her mother."

"Tell nobody that I have lisped a syllable to you. Why, I do not even speak to George about this. An hour ago, it was a secret between me and God,—that I live and move with the one determination that she shall know me one day as I am. Now, Bertha, it is a secret between us three. And you will keep it."

"Indeed I will!" said she; and on the instant, as some stranger came into the room, he bade her good-by, and hurried away.

"Bertha!" said Susie Claridge, pushing back the deep arm-chair in which she had been lying, with its back turned to them, just on the other side of the tall fire-screen. "Bertha!" and she tottered across to her friend, and then sank on the footstool, with her head in Bertha's lap. "Bertha, I heard every word you said, and he"—

"My poor, dear child!" said Bertha, and she bent over her and kissed the sobbing girl.

"Why, how?— I don't know how. Yes, I was here. I think I was asleep, Bertha, and then I heard you laugh, and he laughed; and then I did not know where I was, and then you said something, or he did, I don't know. And it was so pleasant just to hear his voice that I waited one minute before I turned round. Of course it was very weak and very wicked; but I did, Bertha, and then you know — why, then you know — why, what could I do, Bertha, but just lie there and hear the whole?"

"You are a darling child," said Bertha, kissing her, "and he's a hero, if there ever was one. You may forget the whole, my dearie, and I will keep your secret for you. I am good at secrets. Yours is not the first I have had to-night."

And upon that a regiment of people swept in, and at last some of the most distant Watsonville people began to say that it was time to go!

And that was the end of the inauguration meeting of the Deritend Club, so far as the Claridge family was concerned. I remember that we all walked home, and that everybody was very silent; only, as we plodded on in Indian file through the newly fallen snow, I heard Aunt Lois say to her husband,. "My dear Amos, what were you talking about so long with Fanny Gregg?"

And the Doctor, craftiest of men, replied, "Yes, she's a very nice girl indeed. I saw you talking to Clara: is she like her sister?" To which Mrs. Claridge made some unintelligible answer.

And when we came to the stoop of the house, as the Doctor was fumbling for his pass-key, we heard the clock of the college strike twelve. "Christmas morning!" cried Bernard. "Dear Susie, I wish you a merry Christmas and a happy New Year," and with both his hands he took hers, and kissed her. Did their hands hold together a little longer than is usual with the hands of brothers and sisters? I dinna ken. Just then the Doctor found the key, we all tramped into the house and shook the snow from our feet, and Bernard, seizing his candle, rushed directly upstairs, singing, "Adeste fideles, læti triumphantes."

CHAPTER XIV.

CHRISTMAS DAY.

I CALLED that last chapter the Social Revolution, because that phrase came to be a by-word and joke in Bromwich. It had slipped out from some of Mrs. Oelrich's merry talk ; and afterwards, for years, when any thing nice happened which could be traced directly or indirectly to the Deritend Club, we young folks said it belonged to the "Social Revolution:" a horseback ride to Paradise, or a hop on the college lawn at the end of a term, were referred to the "Social Revolution." At last the joke went so far that any girl who meant to have a party that was to be particularly informal and particularly jolly asked you in her notes to a "Social Revolution."

This was all a joke ; but the truth is, that though of course there was no revolution wrought at one particular moment, still from that Christmas eve to this hour, when I write, Bromwich has been a much nicer place to live in than it ever was before. For the sensible and intelligent women of the town, having for once taken direction of its social arrangements in that business of the club, have never let go of them; and so the regulation of the society of the place has never again dropped into the hands of fools or of boys and girls. Of course, in such a place, such women can do just what they choose, if they only set out to in the right way. And the Deritend ladies, finding themselves together from time to time in knots of two or three, engaged in one or another plan which we should hardly have heard of, had they only met under the restricted circumstances of afternoon calls, of neighborhood tea-fights, of parish sociables, or of great evening parties. It might be that two or three of them met by accident at the club rooms, when they had done their shopping; or it might be that when the spring court met here, and the flower of the bar of the State was here, they met from day to day some of the best men we have in public life. The fact that they met each other, and met on common ground, was enough to make them feel at ease in arranging with their husbands and sons what I suppose ought to be called the larger economies of the village, — if economy means the law of living, and not a miserable parsimony.

This is my theory of the thing, and may be all wrong. But I am nine years older than I was that day when Aunt Lois and her committee called on Mr. Gregg and his sons; and I can tell what has happened here since that day. There is a society for planting trees in the streets, and they plant five hundred every year. Last year with their extra money they set up a pretty fountain in the middle of the Common, and a smaller one on that queer triangle in front of the old Elephant tavern. This tree society was formed at the Deritend Club. We have three or four nice companies of amateur actors, each of them under the direction and training of some of the best people of the town and college; and as often as twice a week, every winter, we have an English, French, or German play from them, — plays so well got up and so well patronized that no strolling company of irresponsible blackguards ever seeks foothold in Bromwich. I heard the German company sing Fidelio last week, with Mr. Herman, the minister of the Methodist Church, sitting one side of me, and Professor Baxter, the preacher to the college, on the other, while Jane Edgar, the daughter of the Episcopal minister, was on the stage. None of these clubs would have existed but for the Deritend Club. In the first years of their success, they rented the great ball-room of the "Northern" hotel, and fitted it up with the scenery they wanted for a lecture-room or theatre. Afterwards they didn't know what to do with their money, till somebody suggested a public library, and since that has been in operation the trustees look to the dramatic club to supply it with the periodicals and the literature "of the year."

But I am getting far ahead of my story. Our business is with the Christmas Day which followed the inauguration of the Deritend. Not that I am to tell the fate of every turkey that was roasted that day, or every Marlborough pie that was eaten; but that more than one thing happened on that Christmas of all Christmases which concerned the young people whose fortunes the reader has been following.

Poor Bertha Oelrich had but a hard-working Christmas of it. What with their hospitality at her father's, and their amiability, such days were apt to be hard on her mother and herself. For all the servants wanted to make holiday; and, if Mrs. Oelrich could have had her own way, she would gladly have sent them all to such devices and desires as they wanted to follow, — would have gone into her own kitchen, and sent Gustav Oelrich as good a dinner as he ever saw. But this was a thing he would not permit. So they always entertained a large company at dinner, with such a jury arrangement in the kitchen as breaks the heart of a good housekeeper, and as keeps her daughter in terror all the day long.

On this particular Christmas, Bertha Oelrich had cares and worries of her own. When she came home at midnight from the great party, delighted with its success, but tired — oh, how tired! — to the very corner of the nail on the end of her little finger, — as she stepped into the hall first, of all the party from the carriage, there were sitting four strange women, who rose and curtseyed with savage quaintness — as Bertha said afterwards — first to her and then to her mother. Who in the world were they?

They were John Corkery's wife and his three daughters from Ireland, who had come out to surprise him! They had hoped to arrive on Christmas Day, so as to make the surprise perfect; and they had so far succeeded!

Now Bertha knew that these excellent women existed *in posse*. She knew that by all the received statutes, from the time of Ruth downward, it was, *prima facie*, the business of one of the four, at least, to go where John Corkery went and to stay where he stayed. But she knew also that, in his utter inability to take care of himself for the last fifteen years, this same helpmeet of his had found out long since that he could not take care of her, far less could she take care of him. Bertha had therefore encouraged John to send home from quarter to quarter a large lump of his wages; had read countless letters from "the parties" abroad, acknowledging these lumps; and had satisfied herself that, until John's force of will was decidedly increased, both parties to this contract, the American and the Irish, would be much the happier with the Atlantic between them, —

"Between let ocean roll."

She had gone so far as to read all John's letters "home," with his ready permission. Indeed, he was none too willing to write, unless Miss Bertha put him up to it; and very sure was Miss Bertha that no word nor hint on his part had suggested that these four people should quit service in Armagh for the sake of crossing to Bromwich. Arriving just as they did, when poor John had all a new life before him, Bertha's heart sank, as with the forelook, both of genius and experience, she saw at one flash what the winter was to bring on him and on them. She tried to shut her eyes on what it would bring on her; but she knew in her heart, of course, that the emigration was going to make more trouble to her than to any one of the five. At the moment it seemed as if it were going to work no weal to anybody.

So Bertha's heart sank to the soles of her feet; and, I doubt not, Mrs. Oelrich's to the soles of hers. The Corkery mother and daughters had arrived in the evening train, had come out to the only address they knew of as the abiding place of him to whom they had made this costly and unexpected present, had been received from the coach by one of the jury servants in waiting, — who knew as much of John Corkery as of Zoroaster, and as little, — and now were waiting for advices, for the return from the newborn Deritend Club of the heads of the family.

Poor Bertha! poor Mrs. Oelrich!

It was easy to put them all to bed, but it was quite clear that this Christmas Day would have duties and entertainments all its own.

And so indeed it did. Bertha sent down to John early in the morning explicit and absolute orders that he should come out to the house at once. And he came, — his first visit since his disgrace. Let it be confessed that never was volunteer forced more unwillingly to his duty!

Bertha was determined to be at church with her Sunday-school class. It was the first time our church had ever been opened or decorated for Christmas; and Bertha had spent no end of time and of work in preparing for the carols and the decoration. She was determined to be on hand at home for any contingency in the kitchen, or in the stables even: her poor mother should have all the help she could give her. And now on a day so pre-engaged, — a day, too, which one would have been glad to have for one's self, if one might, for a little of its own blessing to heart and life, — on such a day were these four quaint savages precipitated upon her. She was to persuade John Corkery that he wanted them to come, to persuade them that they were cordially received, and, in the midst of festival and praise, she was to occupy herself in seeing where they were to live, — how they were to live, indeed; and, in a word, to lay the corner-stone of a home.

And Bertha remembered the monk by Geneva who had a vision of the Saviour. "Ah, well!" she said, "if I flinch, where will He go?"

It would have been better, perhaps, for Bertha to have made the emigrants as comfortable as she could till Christmas and New Year's were over, and trusted to the chapter of accidents for their establishment in a home. She could not trust to John Corkery for any such establishment. But it was not Mr. Oelrich's way, nor his wife's, nor his daughter's, to wait much for things to happen, which they could compel. This was a chronic mistake of theirs, "as it seems to me." And also, at this moment, the house, never half large enough for Mr. Oelrich's hospitality, was crowded to the last attic and trunk-room,— double-bedded wherever it could be, Mrs. Oelrich said, — in the preparations that had been made for Christmas. John Corkery, also, was determined that his people should not "squat," as he called it, at Mr. Oelrich's. Whether it were wise or not, therefore, Bertha Oelrich took upon her over-burdened holiday the finding proper lodgings for John Corkery's wife and daughters, and the fit establishment of them in their Western home.

Yes; and I will not say that the details of the enterprise did not add something, at some times, to the zest of her Christmas rejoicing. Mrs. Oelrich did not go to church, — she did not dare to. Gustav Oelrich would not go: no, if he had said what he thought, it would have been that he praised the Lord much more effectively in the one day when the works at the tannery were closed, and he could take the comfort of his home, than he could serve Him in any other ritual. What he did say was, "Go yourself, my darling, and take the boys, if they choose. But nobody in my house shall go to church on Christmas, unless he wants to. I went enough when I was a boy to answer for you all."

And the children did sing the carols nicely, and the festoons and cross over the pulpit did look beautifully, and the choir sang "Adeste fideles" a great deal better than could have been expected; and Bertha sat in her mother's place in the pew, and listened to dear Dr. Prentiss's congratulations happily, without running off more than four times to ask whether, after all, she had not better ask Miss Ellery to lend the Corkerys the cooking-stove that old Mrs. Brant used to have; and whether it would do to have them keep their wood in the backyard at Floyd Street, with that horrid Grattan Court so near them. On the whole, so far as the church went, Bertha enjoyed her service more than if she had read George Herbert all the morning.

CHRISTMAS DAY. 243

But then came dinner; and it was hard work. The cousins were cousins she did not know at all, and they did not know each other. They were cousins of the most silent kind also. Some were cousins of her mother's mother, and some were cousins of her mother's father; and one or two were cousins of Bertha's father, who spoke but little English; and one or two were not cousins at all. Then, it must be confessed, there were hitches in the dinner, into which this chronicle shall not go. And although her father kept up talk and spirits admirably, still Bertha was depressed with the feeling that he was tired and dissatisfied. Poor child! as if it were any affair of hers, whether he were or were not. Every thing seemed to Bertha to drag.

But, after dinner, Mr. Oelrich took off some of the cousins to try the ice on the lake, and Mrs. Oelrich suggested "naps" to the other cousins by way of preparing for a few guests who were expected in the evening. And Bertha, to her joy, found she was alone; and that, after all, she could go down to Floyd Street again, and make sure that the stove had come; and tell the people at Faunce's, at the same time, that these strangers were persons her father was interested in, and that they must have credit, and must not be imposed upon. She knew perfectly well that, if she told her father or mother she was going, she should be prohibited; so she slipped out by the back door to the stable, which she found, as she had hoped, without biped occupants. She harnessed Puss herself, as she had done a hundred times before; she went out by the west avenue, so as not to pass the house, and had all the joy of loneliness and of an escapade, as in the short twilight and early evening she drove rapidly into the village.

But then and there her luck changed. The stove had not come; the wood had not come. There was not a blanket for the improvised beds. John Corkery had been there, — not drunk, as Bertha feared, — but cross beyond language. He had, very clearly, given to all parties a large bit of his mind. He had left them all crying, and had told them they might sleep on the floor for all him; that they had made their beds, such as they were, and that they might lie in them. For his part, he must be at the reading-room; that it was the busiest day in the year there, and that he would not disappoint the managers for a minute, not to set up ten bedsteads. So he had turned, and gone away in a rage.

Bertha rose to the emergency. She was well aware that she had duties elsewhere. She knew also the hopelessness of getting any thing done, in the ordinary methods, on the afternoon of Christmas. But she was indignant at John's cruelty; and she meant to make it good, and she did so. She fell back on the feudal system, which does work marvels when our modern proletariat breaks down. She did not actually wind a horn on the doorstep at the tenement in the house at Floyd Street, but she did what was substantially the same thing. She found the boy at the corner druggist's, — a boy who would have run his shoes off his feet for her father. She sent him here, she sent him there. She soon had Brian O'Donoghue and William Clary in her service. She had Aunt Nancy at the fore, who cared as little for Christmas as she did for Saint Tristrem's Day; regarding them all as so much

"Irish superstition." She told Aunt Nancy what was needed; and Aunt Nancy was very soon telling her. She saw the stove arrive, and in its place; and, when Aunt Nancy put a match in the kindlings, Bertha tore herself away, bade all good-by, and walked up the street, to the corner where she had left the little pony-carriage and Puss. It was dark, but Bertha was not frightened. She knew she should be at home at seven.

Puss was not there! The street was silent and dead, as it can only be at midnight or on a Christmas evening.

Poor Bertha broke down. Had she been such an idiot that she had not fastened Puss? Or had somebody stolen the horse, and gone off on a spree, not knowing what he did? All that was to be learned some time; but now Bertha Oelrich must walk home, and walk home alone.

There was the village at the locks to pass. She had noticed how noisy they were when she came. What a fool she was! Noisy or quiet, she must go home, and must tell her father she was a fool.

And Bertha was, oh, how tired! And however

well her spirit and nerve had held her up while there was some success and achievement, and something still to do, there was no spirit left and no nerve, now that there was no achievement, no success; nothing but failure, and the stupidity of attempting something which she dared not ask leave for, to come home and say she had been all wrong. Every step was like lifting lead for the poor girl. There came over her the thought of the last night, when they had driven home all so jolly and happy. Was she the same girl, and was this the same world?

As she came to the village at the locks, she looked rather timidly to the bridge-corner, to see what might be waiting there: things looked better than she feared. Two men, closely wrapped, and of decidedly forbidding look, were on one side. She could see their forms against the sky. But the other side, the coal-yard side, was clear, not even a wagon fastened there; and Bertha paddled across the street at the moment, that she might take that path, which had at least a roadway between it and these ominous foot-pads. She looked neither to right nor left. She walked as fast as she dared, without running. She came to the bridge, so that she was sure she was passing them. Her foot-fall on it was louder than it had been on the snow. In the moment she heard theirs. They, too, had crossed, they were behind her, they were coming the same way : should she run, should she stand still? She did neither, but walked rapidly on.

This could not last but a moment, she should fall on the ground. But perhaps they would turn off at the corner? Can I walk twenty steps more? And she counted them, — one, two, three, four; one, two, three.

"Miss Oelrich, Miss Oelrich, surely it is Miss Oelrich." It was George Ruther's voice that spoke. And Bertha just succeeded in not screaming, succeeded in not running away, and turned round, and managed to say, "Why, really, you frightened me."

"We ought not to have followed you," said Will Gadsden, who had given her his hand, and could feel how she was trembling. "But I felt sure it was your step, and — and we knew it was by some accident that you were walking."

Bertha then told, still holding out bravely, how her horse had run away, and that she did not dare stop to look for him. The young men proposed a dozen plans, but she would hear to none of them; for they all involved her waiting at one place or another, and she knew papa would be frightened out of his senses if tea-time came without her. Fortunate that tea was late that evening. No, she was quite reassured now, and she would walk home. And so they started. But in a moment Will Gadsden said he was sure he could find something at Bogg's, in which he could carry Miss Bertha home. If they would go on slowly, he would beat up Bogg's quarters, and see. He left them, and they went on together.

Mr. Ruther asked some question further about the accident. But poor Bertha was not herself. She was too tired to say one word. She should not have been forced to do so.

"Oh, it was our poor friend, Corkery. He told you, did he not?"

"Told me! No, he told me nothing. Stay! I did not see him this morning. I looked in at the reading-room, and he was away. I wish I had known. Why did you not send for me? I am sure John is my property as much as yours!"

"Oh, dear! why do I always think that I must 'run the machine,' and then always find that it would do a great deal better if I never touched it? But, as far as that went, I do think it would have been absurd to break up your Christmas holiday too. You have done quite enough for John Corkery."

George Ruther did not understand this hard, short way of speaking in Bertha. In the first place, he did not know how tired she was. In the second place, he did not know that women hold out unchanged to a certain point, and then all their fatigue and nervousness assert themselves at once, and they break right down. Men get tired slowly and by degrees. This was a distinction George Ruther did not then understand.

He plodded stupidly on. "Indeed, Miss Oelrich, it would only have been our part; and, though, of course, I know your plans have been better than mine would have been, — of course you know the neighborhood a great deal better than I, — still I was there, and you were not. I wish you had sent him to me."

"I do not know what your plans would have been," said Bertha, still as hard as Semiramis. "Mine were the worst plans that ever were made, and all broke down together. I found all my people sitting on the floor crying just now, and it is only Aunt Nancy who has put fire on their hearth or bread in their mouths. There's a pretty Christmas in a Christian land. And I, — that is what comes of being born in the purple and fed with a gold spoon, as one of the girls said I was, that I cannot so much as make four wretched women comfortable on the day our Lord was born!"

She was fairly angry now, and hardly knew whom she was talking to.

Now George Ruther, being but eight and twenty years of age, was as ignorant of the nature of woman as if Eve had never been launched into this world. He knew his mother, as he supposed; and he knew his little sister Jane. But for such a change in bearing and speech as came over poor Bertha, now that she was "dead beat," disappointed, tired, and all broken down, George Ruther was as utterly unprepared as he would have been to see her change into a white doe and disappear in the shrubbery.

He did not know what to say, and he did not know what to do. He felt more like crying than any thing else; but, being a man, he thought he would not cry. For a minute they walked on in silence, and then he said what was uppermost, as he was, indeed, a little apt to, —

"I do not see why you say that, Miss Bertha. I never saw anybody who was as efficient as you are, or brought so much to pass. I am sure I have a right to say so."

"I wish you would not say such things," Mr. Ruther. "I say them to myself a great deal too much, and they make me the vain, foolish goose that I am. A girl who knows better than her father, and knows better than her mother, and then has to leave William Clary and Aunt Nancy to do her work for her, has to see them do what she cannot begin to do, and then paddle home on foot in the darkness and mud and snow," — and here Bertha viciously kicked a stubborn frozen clod out of her path, — " a girl who must go home and tell her father that she is a goose, and tell her mother that she is a fool, should not be told that she is very efficient." And she fairly sobbed in her vexation.

Ruther had admired this bright, merry, wide-awake child of good fortune, from the first moment that he saw her. She understood every thing so readily at half a word, she joined in so precisely at the right moment, she had consecrated her life by the same principles that were the life of his, in every thing she had seemed to him a wonder and a delight. But she never had seemed to him so charming as she did now, when she was all dejected and broken. He would have been glad to take the poor tired child in his arms, and carry her home to her mother, and ask leave to carry her so for ever and a day.

But such are not the customs of the nineteenth century.

So Ruther blundered on, as best he could, in the forms suggested by this century, which thinks it believes more in talk than in symbols.

"Well, who thinks he can do every thing? You cannot put up a stove, and you are distressed because you have failed. But I do not believe that your father could put it up any better than you can. I am sure I am not distressed because I cannot dress the pulpit with flowers, as you did this morning ; or knit Bertie Joy his mittens, which you gave to him this morning."

"There it is," said Bertha, still on her "bender." "Knitting and flowers ! That is just about what I am fit for, and what I ought to learn to be satisfied with."

Poor Ruther could have bitten his tongue out, to think that it should have served him in illustrations so futile. But it is of the nature of such a man as he to stick to the idea on which he has started, and to compel others at least to understand ; and so he manfully persisted.

"Well, if you do not like that instance, take a dozen others. I am talking of the woman who bullied Krieshammer till she got the tassels he had promised ; who audited nineteen several bills for furniture and carpets ; who discovered the mistake in Worth's accounts, which nobody else had seen ; the woman who was never one minute late in twenty meetings of the Executive Committee, whose records never were corrected, who never lost her temper when every one else was cross, and who made peace between all quarrelsome people, so that they forgot that they had quarrelled. I do not think it is fair for that woman to say that she is a cipher, and for one I will not stand it," said he, laughing, as if to excuse his earnestness.

Bertha herself was a little startled. Was it possible that anybody cared for her, and watched her so closely that he knew what Mr. Ruther was saying of her, every syllable of which she knew in her own heart was true?

"Perhaps, then first she understood
Herself how wondrously endued."

She paused for a few seconds in her turn, and then said, as the great over-ruling genius of Modern Society dictated, —

"You are very kind, Mr. Ruther." She was frightened, and she did not dare trust herself to fight any longer, nor, indeed, to say one word more.

"I tell the truth," said Ruther, warmed and excited, and quite beyond the guard he had placed upon himself in all the walk until now, as in all their intercourse before. "I tell the truth. I have wondered and wondered, from day to day, where and how a person so tender and gentle as you, so accomplished and bright as you, so unselfish and considerate as you, so necessary in home life and so perfect in it, came to have this capacity for affairs which I never saw in any man, and the intuitive knowledge of character which comes to your help at every moment."

He was a little frightened now, but Bertha said no word. They walked on, and then he added: "I have said it. I have said more than I should have dared say, had not I been all overset and beside myself to see any one in distress and in tears who is so inexpressibly dear to me as you are. O Miss Bertha, I may well say this here, where I have walked almost every day for the last two months, in the hope that I might at least touch my hat to you, or possibly meet you in walking; where there is not a corner of the road, but I associate it with you. I had rather say this here than anywhere,— say what you please to me."

— "All right, old fellow!" This was the cry — not of Bertha, as the reader may suppose by accident, but of Will Gadsden arriving from behind with Dan Bogg's horse, in Dan Bogg's lumber-wagon. "All right! Bogg was only too gracious. See, Miss Bertha, there are two buffaloes for you to sit upon; and even a milking-stool for Mr. Ruther, if he drives."

Mr. Ruther could have choked Will Gadsden, though he loved him. But he lifted Bertha to the wheel and the rude seat; and her hand did not press his, fair reader, — no, nor linger in it one instant. It was a stone hand. She said something to Gadsden, — she did not know what, far less do I. Ruther made Gadsden sit at her side, mounted to the milk-stool as bidden, and drove as if he were in triumph to the avenue and to Mr. Oelrich's door.

Then Will Gadsden offered to lift Bertha down from the cart; and George Ruther stood at the horse's head, to be sure that he did not start. Bertha jumped lightly to the porch, gave her hand frankly to Will, and by this time was able to thank him. Then, with perfectly clear voice, she spoke into the darkness: —

"Fasten him by the chain, Mr. Ruther; and I will send Conrad, or somebody, to take him home. You must come in, — pray come in, Mr. Ruther! I shall never get through with papa, unless my two knights help me through."

George Ruther was under the lantern by this time. And, as he looked into her eyes, — all running over with tears as they were, — he saw all that any man had a right to ask, although she did not give him a hand nor say one word beside.

She left the two gentlemen to their own devices in the hall, and, for herself, ran up to her own room.

The two gentlemen introduced themselves into the drawing-room, and, in the crowd of frightened and uneasy cousins, Mrs. Oelrich did not, at the first moment, understand that they came with Bertha, — which, indeed, both of them had tact enough not to proclaim. To this moment she did not know that her daughter was out of the house. To say truth, Mrs. Oelrich was at this first moment not sorry to have allies so wide-awake and ready to assist in the entertainment of her Christmas party, which, as the reader has seen, had in it certain elements of friction, not to say of incongruity.

It did not at the instant occur to her that there was one additional element of incongruity introduced by Will Gadsden's arrival. Wanting to lighten up the evening, if she could, she had despatched Conrad with a note to Mrs. Claridge, asking if some of them could not come over, and bidding Conrad wait and bring whoever would come. The summons had been answered by the arrival of Dr. Claridge, Aunt Lois, Susie, and myself, who write these words ; and the bustle of our reception was but just over, and we were scattered with different cousins, all more or less taciturn or frightened, in the conservatory, in the billiard-room, or in the library, when the two young men entered, in manner as has been described.

I doubt if Mrs. Oelrich quailed when, after five minutes, it did occur to her that Will Gadsden and Susie Claridge might be glad not to be under the same roof. No, I am sure she did not quail. "It is their look-out," she said to Gustav, "and not mine. There are six rooms here; and, if they choose to run against each other, I certainly am not to blame. Let the feast go on!" And it went on,— with all the more vivacity for the incursion of these six new revellers.

When, half an hour afterwards, Bertha Oelrich came into the room at tea-time, she was radiantly beautiful. I had admired her afar off, ever since I came to college at Bromwich; but I had never seen her with the expression both of pride and tenderness, of power and of gentleness, which shone through her face and moved in every movement now. No, I do not know how she had dressed herself, — do not ask me! — but it was some dress of festival, which yet was a dress of the fireside. She moved with the lighthearted step of a woman who is perfectly happy and perfectly at home. And yet her face was thoughtful, while it was glowing with life: you wondered what she was going to say, and yet she said hardly a word. I know I looked on with wonder, and I could see that her mother looked on with equal wonder, — and, shall I say, with pride unconcealed. Bertha gave her hand to such new-comers as were in the large drawing-room. George Ruther was not there. Then she attached herself to the most irresolute and terrified cousin of all, one of the kind whom I have spoken of as not even a cousin, and, beginning by showing him the pictures in a copy of "Punch" which had just come from the mail, soon had him laughing and talking about the blunders of his college life ; and in ten minutes that little fool had persuaded himself that this matchless woman had fallen desperately in love with him.

Before long Mrs. Oelrich gathered a part of her forces in the large parlor, and seated them in a long irregular oval. They were to play at "Consequences." The machinery of the game was simply enough arranged ; and a young cousin of fifteen, who had played it at the academy, and knew all about it, and whispered to her new friends things which would be very funny to write, had the collection of the papers and the reading aloud of the results. We were all good-natured, some of us were inspired. Every one was under the glamour of Bertha's queenly good-spirits. George Ruther was not in the room. He was explaining a cabinet of fossils to a cousin who was a little deaf, but was interested in natural history. Under the regular sequence of the game, we had all sorts of absurd complications; the young folks sitting in the inner row to hear the vaticinations which came forth from the half oracles which they had deposited in the sacred tripods. These tripods were in fact hats, brought in from the hall. At the last moment, a tall shy gentleman from Bremen brought in Susie Claridge and placed her in a chair, behind which he stood. It was too late for her to see that Will Gadsden was directly opposite her. No matter if he were. Around the oval hovered a body of the older people, and gradually the laughter and surprise of the noisy game brought everybody into the room.

Well, we had the usual reverses of fortune: —

"General Butler" — *and* "Pocahontas" — *met* "in a balloon" — "at the foot of Gamaliel." *He said*, "Do you smoke?" *She said*, "Not much." *And the consequence was* "she became an archangel."

Of course we all laughed, and the children stamped; and Miss Gilbert, encouraged with the success of her game, went boldly on: —

"Jefferson Davis"—*and* "Rosa Bonheur"—*met* "in quod"—"at Antietam." *He said*, "I defy you in your teeth." *She said*, "Does your mother know you're out?" *The consequence was* "they went where glory waits them."

New applause, new surprise at the aptness of the answers; and so the game went on through a dozen similar repartees, till some demon presiding over such chances ordered that, in drawing from the hats, Miss Gilbert—who did not know three people in the town by name, far less did she know the relations that bound one to another—read as loudly and freely as she had read the others: —

"Mr. William Gadsden"—*and* "Miss Susan Claridge"—*met* "in a grog-shop"—"by the side of the canal." *He said*, "I love you." *She said*, "I hate you." *And the consequence was* "he took strychnine and died."

Fortunately the younger boys and girls, as ignorant as Miss Gilbert, all screamed and clapped as before. Whether Will Gadsden's hair turned white I did not know. Whether Susie Claridge sank through the floor I did not know. I looked straight at the piano for an instant, and in one instant more we all sprang to our feet at a terrible smash. One of the great Japanese vases, which stood on a tripod behind Miss Clarke's chair, had fallen.

It is my belief, and will be till I die, that Gustav Oelrich himself kicked it over, to make the diversion which was so necessary. Any way, his object was accomplished.

That night we "played consequences no more."

CHAPTER XV.

TWO BY TWO.

"WOULD you rather go home, my darling?" said Mrs. Claridge tenderly to Susie, in a side-room, after the company had broken into groups again. "It is very hot here."

"Oh, no! dear mamma, don't be anxious about me. I'll be all right in a minute. I will go into Bertha's room for a half an hour, and when I come down I will be as right as ever. Of course, — well, I should not have come, if I had known he would be here; but such things must happen, and I may as well face them. But was any thing ever quite so bad?" And the poor girl cried again, and ran away.

"Of course you know, my dear child," said Mrs. Oelrich to Mrs. Claridge, when she found her, "that when I sent for you I had no dream that he was to be here. You know how much he and Mr. Ruther are together, and they came in without a whisper of an invitation. I am so sorry."

In a moment more, Will Gadsden was at her side. "Dear Mrs. Oelrich, of course you know that I did not know she was here. I have schooled myself to that quite too thoroughly to make a mistake now. I am so sorry I came! But now I will thank you for your hospitality and be gone — as soon as I can find my hat!" — this almost quizzically, as he looked back into the broken oval.

"Thank you, my dear Will," — this with intention. "But, so far as I can think, I think you had better not go. There are six rooms here, and I will trust your tact. It will trouble the Doctor and all, if you go away." This she said almost eagerly.

"Just as you say," said he; and he called a stout boy, and engaged him at checkers in the billiard-room.

Susie did not take the half-hour she asked for, in which to recover her balance. I was standing and talking with Mrs. Oelrich when the two girls entered the room together, and never shall I forget the impression they made on me. I did not know then all this that I have been telling you now, and I could not have explained what I saw. But here was Bertha radiantly beautiful, as I have said, thoughtful and cheerful, as if she were going to conquer the world, or see some one else conquer it. And Susie, if she had been crying, showed no signs of it. She was very pale, but very lovely, as to my eye she always was; and, though she was not touching Bertha, I believe any one who loved her as I did would have had the feeling that I had, that she was clinging to her for strength, and relying on her for the rest of the evening. I think she was.

And for a long time, indeed, the two girls kept together. Perhaps they had bound themselves to do so. They stood by the fire together, they sang a duet together; they sat on the sofa together, riding on their feet some little girls, who were begging not to be sent to bed. But of a sudden a servant beckoned to Bertha from the door, and she knew that she must run into the dining-room to take order about the supper, and ran out, leaving Susie alone.

Susie turned to a shy girl who was looking at engravings at the table by her side, and asked her if she had been into the conservatory, and if she would not like to go there? The shy girl was glad to go anywhere, where there would be no one to look at her. In the conservatory there was a specimen of *Barneveldtia verticillata*, which had taken this Christmas evening to show for the first time the glory of its magnificent blossom; and Susie gladly took her shy neighbor to see it. The little girl warmed under her kindness, and Susie herself was quite at ease with her again. They fell to talking about their luck with smilax and with ferns, and at last Susie dragged her round under the plant platforms into a dark little den there is, to show her how the gardener was striking some cuttings. Susie was just as much at home in every corner of that house as Bertha herself was.

When they reappeared in the conservatory, they came out upon a group who had been brought in to see the Barneveldtia. Next to Susie, as she stept out of the little door, was Will Gadsden, who had brought in Sarah Clarke, after taking the precaution to look in and to make certain that no one was there. Others had followed them, so that the little pathway in the greenhouse was crowded full.

"Is not it lovely, too lovely?" cried the gushing Miss Clarke to Susie. "How wonderfully those purple stamens bend down over the white! and do you see, Mr. Gadsden, that darling little cross in the middle? I never saw any thing so lovely."

"I knew you would like it," said Will, bravely; "and now I will leave you with the ladies, and make my good-bys."

"So early, Mr. Gadsden?" said Susie Claridge. "I hope we don't frighten you away." And she put out her hand as frankly as Sarah Clarke could have done.

"Thank you, indeed," gasped Will, choking hard as he spoke. But Miss Clarke fortunately was again possessed by her guardian genius, and began an aria in prose on petioles and filaments and pores in the anthers, which flowed on as easily as some smooth river.

And Will did not go. Miss Clarke, if she thought of the reason, thought that her own eloquence had held him. In a moment more, however, she made a dash at the more distant part of the conservatory. "That is Fellowsia, I know it is Fellowsia, and the fructification on the fronds is the most curious thing in the world." She rushed forward, followed by the train of ladies, for whose passage in the narrow pathway Will pressed back as best he could. The frightened girl, without any known name, who was Susie's companion, was swept away in the throng; and Susie in the doorway, and Will pressed against an orange-tree, were left together to bring up the rear.

"Will you give me one word, Mr. Gadsden?"

"Will I?" said he; and with two steps he led her to the orchid-house, which at this season had no special attractions for the enthusiasts.

"I have been upstairs, resting in Bertha's room, since — since Mr. Oelrich broke his jar," said Susie, very pale, but trying to smile; "and I have had a chance to think a little. Still I should not have said any thing, but that we happened to meet again here. And now, as we have met, I want to say this. We are not living in a book:

we are living in Bromwich, which is a very small and very common-place town. If you must leave this conservatory because I am here, you must leave any other room that I happen to be in. We shall have scenes all the time, and very foolish scenes. Do not let us be such fools as that: we should only make each other uncomfortable; and that is the last thing that I want, and I am sure the last that you want. Can't we stand at ease, as I think you soldiers say?"

And she succeeded in keeping down her tears even, she was so resolute, — yes, she succeeded in looking into his eyes, which were brimming and running over. Meanwhile, Miss Clarke led her train out through the further door into the billiard-room; and no one but the frightened girl without a name missed Susie or Will, — least of all Miss Clarke, who was instructing Mr. Hausmann about pollen.

"'At ease' is a good deal to say," said Will, trying to smile. "But I am quite a good actor, you know, of old," he added after a pause. "Whatever you think best, that I will do, or will try to do, as well as I can. It would be easier for me to leave town once for all, than to be dodging you from this drawing-room or that sidewalk."

"Oh, don't say that!" said Susie, more impulsively than she meant. And then, controlling herself: "Don't let an accident or a set of accidents interfere with studies, and a plan which you have carefully arranged. I can be as careful as you," she added with some pride, "and we shall not trouble each other often."

"Oh, don't say that!" cried he, a little off guard, but still using her own words with a tone that showed he used them. "We shall never trouble each other at all now, — now that we understand each other," he added very sadly.

"We do not understand each other," said Susie, bravely, "unless we meet and part as friends. I believe that is what I set out to say, only I blundered."

She gave him both her hands, and he took them with a surprised and reverent courtesy, as if an image of the Madonna had stretched out its hand to him, when he was on his knees in prayer.

"If you can say that," said he, "you do more for me than I knew that any man or woman could do, when I came to see that flower. You do more for me than words can tell. This is a Christmas present, indeed. And I shall always be grateful, Miss Claridge." And he dropped the cold hands, because he would not trust himself to say one word more.

Both of them were silent. After what had passed, neither could make a movement, without this certain misapprehension. Perhaps neither of them wanted to say any thing. But after a minute Will had a feeling of his own high chivalry, that he was bound now to address her as any other man would; and, with a distinct feeling that he must act his part of "friend" as well as he could, he thought up something to say, and said, "How beautiful Miss Oelrich is this evening!" It was a good cue to give, and in her heart Susie thanked him.

"Perfectly beautiful! It is wonderful to see her strength and spirit, for she has had a terribly hard day of it."

"Did she tell you"— Will began, and then he doubted whether he would speak of her little accident. He botched the sentence a little, and said, "Did she tell you about her new Irish friends?"

"She did not, but Mrs. Oelrich did. Dear Bertha! if all Ireland appeared on the lawn tomorrow morning, they would all be comfortable in tents before night. She understands Mr. Ruther's maxim, and knows how to 'lend a hand.'"

If any thing could put Susie at her ease, in a conversation which was so embarrassing, it was to talk of Bertha to some one who appreciated her. Will had not hit badly in choosing his subject.

"She knows how to 'lend a hand,'" said he, "because she forgets herself. 'She looks out, and not in.' That is another of their Wadsworth mottoes. And as anybody knows, who knows Ruther as well as I do, or knows Bertha as well as you do, this is for both of them, because they 'look up, and not down.' And, as he spoke, he pointed into the drawing-room, where, after the loyal service of this eventful evening, Bertha and George were rewarded by being at last together; and where they could see that he was talking with all his might, and Bertha listening with all her heart, unconscious of every thing around.

And Will Gadsden and Susie Claridge were both more at ease for the moment than they had thought they could ever be in each other's company. For the moment both of them stood silent, and enjoyed the consciousness of ease. Silence is golden, indeed, when it comes at such times and after such storms. Nay, for the moment, neither of them was thinking of self.

"I believe we are both thinking of the same thing," said Susie, timidly, but fairly with a smile upon her face.

"Are we?" said he, and he started. "I do not dare tell you what I am thinking of. You will say I have no right."

"I am thinking of those two, — that it is a pleasure to see them together, and think of them together. Bertha is very strong, and she is very well-balanced; but she is not strong enough to be alone, and I like to see her with a friend so strong as he."

"Though I know him so well," said Will, "Bertha is the only person he never speaks of to me, except in the most casual way. And I believe he worships her as she passes him in the street."

Then Will was frightened, for he knew that he would have said this to no living being but to Susie Claridge. And he was frightened to think he had dared say it to her.

"We must not talk of such friends," said she, smiling again, "if we cannot help match-making. But I cannot well tell you what a help Bertha has been to me, and is to all of us."

"It is an eclogue we are singing in," said Will; "for I cannot well tell you what a help Ruther has been to me and to all of us. He teaches me, — no, he does not teach me, that is the glory of it, — I believe he inspires me. If I am with him, I forget all about myself, and am not torturing myself with questions. I do not feel my pulse. I do not inquire about my sins. I do not take credit for my smart speeches. I do not distress myself about my blunders. And I believe it is the same with the workmen down in the repair-shop. There is not a man of them but Ruther makes more manly; and there is not a man of them who would not die for him, as I would. O Miss Susie, it is every thing for a poor dog who has lived such a life as I have, and dragged through as much dirt as I have grovelled through, to be honored by the confidence of such a man!"

Susie's eyes flashed fire. Was she inspired? Perhaps. Any way, she did not mean to go round again in that same weary round with him. "Then there is one of his mottoes that you do not learn, Mr. Gadsden. You do not learn from him to '*look forward, and not back.*'"

"Susie!"

"If you did, Will, you would not come here and talk to me as if I were always remembering your past, and had no eye for your present. You would not meet my father as if he could not forget as well as forgive. You would not, Will, compel me to say what I am bold enough and wild enough to say now."

"O Susie!" he said again; and he tried to say something more, but she would not let him.

"No, Will," said she, "it is not you only who have been in a false position. Since the club last night, I think my position has been harder than yours. For I have been living, — you must hear me out — with all the disgrace and terror of an eavesdropper. I was behind the fire-screen in the club parlor when you were talking with Bertha; and, Will, I heard every syllable you said to her." And the poor, pale girl blushed fire, and looked in his face no longer, but hung her head, and looked upon the ground.

"Then you heard God's own truth for once," cried Will, "and I should be glad to publish it to all these people. I would not have dared say it, — no, not for years — to you; but, now it is said, I say it again, and will say it again, as long as you will let me. And I will ask no answer; but, answer or no answer, I will love you, Miss Susie, I will honor you, and I will try to serve you till I die."

The girl looked up and looked down. She looked up again and looked down again. She looked up, and tried to speak, and her lips only trembled.

"I make you wretched," said he, "and you are trying to spare me misery."

"No," said the girl, bravely, "you do not make me wretched. I am trying to say that I am glad this veil is rent, and that you will take even as feeble help as mine for what is before you. What

I wanted to say I said before: if you will 'look forward, and not backward,' I will."

"And I want to say — what I said once before to your mother — that if there is a saint this side heaven that saint is you."

"You must not say such things as that, till you know much more of saints and of me than you know now. And now you must not talk to me any longer: you must give me your arm, and take me out of this conservatory to go and speak to Bertha."

"Might we tell Miss Gilbert that we are friends?" said Will, fairly laughing now.

She gave him her arm, as proudly as a queen. They crossed to Bertha, who for once was so absorbed in what she was saying to George Ruther that she did not know they came up to her. But Will boldly touched her arm, and said, "Miss Bertha, we have come to say that Miss Susie tells me not to 'look back, but to look forward,' and that she is going to 'lend a hand.'"

Bertha's face blazed with light. "Am I relieved from my promise, Will?"

"You may tell her what you choose," said he. "I will have no secrets from her any longer."

"May I tell him, Bertha, that you have no secrets from me?" said George Ruther.

"After what you said to papa," said Bertha, laughing, "you may say any thing to such children as these two are." And then, in presence of the whole company, of whom, at least, Miss Clarke and Miss Gilbert and I myself were looking on with some wonder at this excited talk and its dumb show, she threw her arms around poor dear Susie's neck, and kissed her and kissed her again and again.

"Christmas, indeed!"

CHAPTER XVI. AND LAST.

BROMWICH TO-DAY.

AH, well! This is all well-nigh nine years ago, as I write these words. Perhaps I need not have written so much of the joy and triumph of those young lives. But all four of these young people would say to you, if you went into Ruther's house or to Gadsden's, that all the history of the beginning of the New Crusade was mixed in with the history of their discovering each other. They would say that they could not tell the one part without the other, and so they would excuse me for telling it so. For them these have been bright years, indeed,—years of unselfish love,— years of happy homes, full of work for others and prayer for others,—years of light and life and success. Meanwhile this little Bromwich of ours has been going through one and another experiment in social life, all of which have ended in making us love this place as we love no other, and talking of it in ways that other people think absurd. When the Governor offered Will a seat on the Supreme Bench last spring, — and Will was only thirty-three, — Will thought, and Susie thought, that they could not move away from Bromwich. And when George took Bertha to Philadelphia for the winter, — it is now three years ago, — she said, and I believe, that she was homesick long before they came home. She says, and I guess it is true, that we get more out of life than most groups of six thousand people do.

For the particular matter with which the Crusade began, it makes little difference to us whether the county vote for license, as it sometimes does, or whether it vote against it. With us the habit of "perpendicular drinking," to cite that convenient phrase again, is broken up. The college-boys who have it when they come forget it; an occasional fast young clerk or machinist, who comes to Bromwich from Toledo or Cleveland or Pittsburg, either finds us too slow and leaves us, or gets interested in something which is going on, and forgets his old stimulus. Ruther and his set have been for ever starting some scheme or another for amusing their Irish and French and German work-people, lifting up the level of their life, and making them look for something more than they used to. They had penny readings, where the Irish newspapers, and, in the war, the German accounts of victories, were read aloud night after night, in clouds of bad tobacco. They even consented to dances, where men and women brought back old memories, now of Connaught and now of Hanover, and were none the worse, perhaps, because for the moment it seemed as if they were at home. Out of their flower-shows, down at the reading-room, grew gardening such as we never dreamed of in Bromwich before; and your thorough gardener needs no stimulus nor amusement, but his flowers. Before a great while they had a homestead club running; and now George tells me there is not a married man on the railroad payroll, nor in the Locks Village, nor at the tanneries at Faff's, but who owns his own cottage, with a quarter-acre, at least, of land. George laughs when he says it, and says Bertha might go fishing at midnight from the bridge-rail with nobody to terrify her, — that everybody else, indeed, not so romantic as she, would be a-bed.

For the Deritend Club, as I said, it is twice as large, in rooms and in numbers, as it was in those doubtful days of the opening. We try not to be aristocratic. None the less do we have that bad name. But we have done a good many democratic things. The public library is our thunder, as I said; the theatre and the three dramatic clubs came from us also; the tree-planting was ours, and the Horticultural Society. All the Lyceum courses rely on the "Deritend" to sell their tickets for them; and the cotillon-parties every winter, which are very democratic, are under our distinguished patronage. For all this, when Mike Mellen at last left the "Elephant," because he could not sell whiskey enough there to pay his rent, — after the house had been vacant twelve months, some of the carriage-builders and blacksmiths out in Front Street took the whole house, and opened it in opposition to the Deritend for a club-house. They called their club "The People's Club," and explained at much length that they were not going to be exclusive as we were. They also abolished liquor, of course: there was one nuisance the less. They made some rules that we thought very strict, and they refused to make some which we think very necessary. All the same, they have flourished in their fashion, and we in ours, and all the more for a little healthy rivalry. To give them their due, they went right into clean politics, which we had been afraid of; and they blew the county "Ring" sky-high. They turned the Robbinses out, who had kept the county almshouse for ten or twelve centuries, and put in Martin and his wife. They voted a heavy tax on the property of the town for water, and brought down the death rate of the town from twenty-eight to twenty-two by bringing the water in. It is a harum-scarum, talkee-talkee sort of place, is the "People's Club;" but it must be owned that it takes, and that it has done a great deal of good in its way.

Meanwhile, there has been less quarrelling in Bromwich than in any place of its size I ever heard of. Every Monday morning I find all the ministers, the Irish priest included, in the club-room. I rather think, if the truth were told, that the Union Revival was born there. I know the "Provident Society," which undertook to feed all the poor people, was ; and that society lasted till the discovery that, except poor blind old Nydia Mœonides, after she lost her hearing, and had a stroke of "numb palsy," there were no poor people in the town.

Our whole history has been one illustration of the truth of Aunt Lois's dictum : that, in the social order of such a place as ours, the best men and women can do just what they choose, if they will only work together. She says that the men cannot do much alone, and that the women cannot do much alone. She says that both together they will not do much, unless they aim high. But, if they find out what they want, she says they can do what they want, if they will overcome evil with good. The success of "the Deritend" was in the substitution for the stimulus of bad liquor the stimulus of the highest and best society. The success of the "reading-room" and its adjuncts was in the bringing together of hard-working and hard-worked men and women, who had been taught to soak and smoke alone. The new life of the town has come, as the town has found out that "society" is possible whenever everybody will determine to give and take, and that the best society is possible whenever the seniors do not desert their posts, and leave social arrangements to boys and to girls.

The loyal resolve of everybody to live in the common life was the inspiration and the success of

THE NEW CRUSADE.

THE END.

Cambridge: Press of John Wilson & Son.

www.ingramcontent.com/pod-product-compliance
Lightning Source LLC
Chambersburg PA
CBHW031345230426
43670CB00006B/437